Wicked Jurupa Valley

Wicked Jurupa Valley

Murder & Misdeeds in Rural Southern California

Kim Jarrell Johnson

The History Press

Published by The History Press
Charleston, SC 29403
www.historypress.net

Front cover, top: The temporary pedestrian bridge over the Santa Ana River, 1916. *Courtesy of the Ida Parks Condit family. Front cover, bottom:* From a postcard featuring a view of the Rubidoux area taken from Mount Rubidoux. *Courtesy of Steve Lech.*

First published 2012

Manufactured in the United States

ISBN 978.1.60949.520.6

Library of Congress CIP data applied for.

Contents

Acknowledgements

As always, very generous people in the local history community have helped me with this book. Nancy Wenzel made the mistake of agreeing to read my stories and made many helpful suggestions. Steve Lech, who has done extensive reading on Gordon Northcott and the Wineville Chicken Coop Murders, generously shared his time and photos with me. Steve also opened up his postcard collection for my use and created the map of Jurupa Valley used in this book. Kevin Hallaran at the Riverside Metropolitan Museum made many searches for me in that institution's collections. While his searches were not always successful, I appreciate the time he took to look. Jim Hofer, the Riverside County archivist, was also very helpful, and I appreciated his assistance as I searched through old assessors' records.

My daughter Corinne is an English major, and she often was roped in to read a story with fresh eyes or to help me find a better word than what my mind or the computer could provide. My daughter Elyse also provided another set of fresh eyes and read several stories for me. Both daughters often got to hear about these stories and their cast of characters as I discovered them, and their tolerance is appreciated.

As always, without my husband, this book would not have been possible. He smoothed over my lack of computer skills and, especially in that frantic last-minute rush to get things done, was the brains behind the entire operation. He is also my most trusted editor and fit in many

The intersection of Mission Boulevard and Riverview Drive in 1938 was a country crossroads, not a major intersection like it is today. This photo was taken because of the automobile accident that is visible in the picture.

readings during his own busy days. There are no words to express my appreciation and love.

And, to everyone who asked if the story of the Wineville Chicken Coop Murders would be in this book, I can finally say, “Yes, it is!”

Introduction

Jurupa Valley is located in inland Southern California, and while it is a new city that just incorporated on July 1, 2011, it has a long history of settlement, starting with the Jurupa Rancho, which was created in 1838. However, not all of modern-day Jurupa Valley was located within the boundaries of the Jurupa Rancho. That part of our city located north of Bellegrave Avenue was government land that in the 1800s and early 1900s was available for homesteading.

The modern city of Jurupa Valley is made up of a number of different communities that sprung up as the area was subdivided and settled. A map of Jurupa Valley has been included that shows the communities, landmarks and roads which are referred to in the stories in this book to help readers orient themselves with where the various events took place.

Much of the information used in these stories came from local newspapers. During the time frame that most of the stories in this book occurred, Jurupa Valley did not have a newspaper and certainly never had a daily newspaper. However, Riverside, the big city to the south, had several daily papers through the years. These newspapers, primarily the *Riverside Daily Press* and the *Riverside Enterprise*, also covered the news that happened in the Jurupa Valley area. Articles were also found in the *Los Angeles Times* that provided information for stories. It became obvious, particularly in the earlier years, that the *Los Angeles Times* was getting its information through a relationship with the *Daily Press*. The stories in

This 1890 map of Southern California shows West Riverside (which is what the area that now includes Rubidoux and Glen Avon was called then), just north of the city of Riverside. *Courtesy author.*

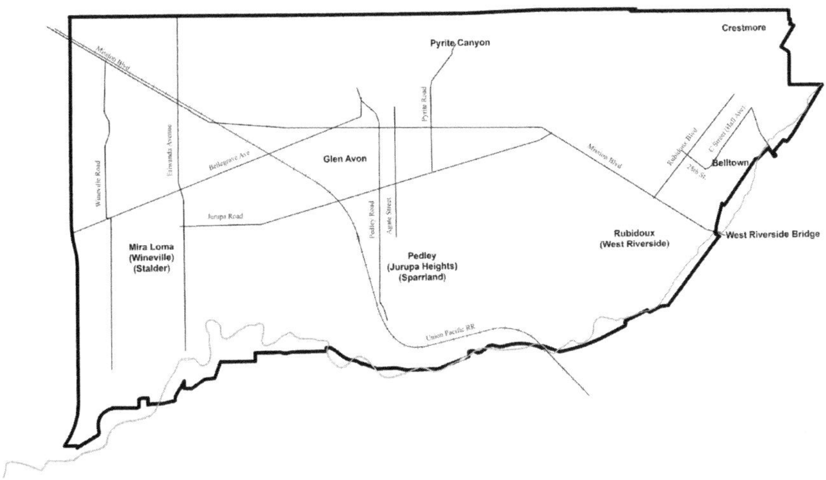

This map of Jurupa Valley shows the communities, streets and landmarks that are featured in the stories in *Wicked Jurupa Valley*. *Courtesy Steve Lech.*

both were usually almost identical, and a mistake made in an article in the *Daily Press* was almost always repeated in the *Los Angeles Times*.

The *Daily Press* was an afternoon paper and the *Enterprise* a morning paper. Much to my surprise, I found that articles about the same incident in the two newspapers at times contained very different, if not contradictory, information. When the facts differed, I tried, as much as possible, to confirm the facts with other sources, such as census records or community directories. I found additional information by talking to other local historians, checking for information in online databases and in local history books. I also reached out to descendants of the people in these stories when possible. To the best of my ability, I have reported the facts of the cases in this book accurately. However, I am always open and willing to look at new information and welcome it from anyone who would like to contact me.

Names and their spellings were another thing that was often not reported correctly in the newspapers. Many times just initials were given for first and middle names, making it hard to trace the people mentioned in the newspaper articles in other sources. Names of Mexican origin, both first and last, seemed to be spelled phonetically. I have used the name and spelling that is most likely correct, based on my research.

It was not my intention to produce a scholarly work but instead an entertaining book that gives the reader a flavor of the old days and some of the interesting characters and events in Jurupa Valley history. However, I have tried to include enough information so that, if you so choose, you can do additional research on your own. If you would like to do further reading on Jurupa Valley history, I have included a selected bibliography of other books that are available. Some may only be available in the reference section of local libraries, but others are more recent publications, available in local stores and online.

Chapter 1

Infamous Chicken Coop Murders Still Fascinate

Some murders are so infamous that books are written, movies are made and, almost one hundred years later, people are still morbidly fascinated with the details. Such is the case of Gordon Stewart Northcott and the most infamous murder case in the history of Jurupa Valley—the Wineville Chicken Coop Murders.

Gordon Northcott was born in Canada in 1906 to George and Louise Northcott. Gordon had one sister named Winnifred who was sixteen or seventeen years older than him. His sister married the same year that he was born. Between the two births, Louise Northcott had five other pregnancies, only one of which resulted in a child that lived for any length of time. That little boy, Willie, died when he was just five years old. It was the traumatic loss of numerous children and, particularly, the devastating loss of Willie that may have at least partially driven Louise's unnatural attachment to her son Gordon. Gordon was her true love, far more than her husband, her daughter or her grandchildren. In her eyes, he could do no wrong and had to be protected at any cost.

In 1924, Gordon and his parents moved to Los Angeles. Gordon was approximately nineteen years old at the time. There has been some speculation that they moved because Gordon was already getting into trouble due to his desire for young boys. However, there is no proof that the family moved for that reason.

In the spring of 1926, George Northcott bought three acres of vacant land in Wineville, a rural area in Riverside County. The plan was for Gordon to start a chicken ranch on the property. By this point, Gordon's parents had to know that Gordon sexually abused boys. He was charged with mistreating a young boy in 1925, but the case was dismissed due to lack of evidence. Did his parents think that sending him to the rural area of Wineville would remove him from contact with young boys? Whatever his parents were thinking, the purchase of the Wineville property simply gave Gordon a more isolated place to satisfy his desires.

In the summer of 1926, before any improvements had been made to the Wineville property, Gordon decided to visit his older sister and her family in Saskatoon, Saskatchewan, Canada, under the guise of needing someone to help him get the chicken ranch going. However, Gordon did not mention his need for help with the chicken ranch to his sister's family. Instead, he talked his thirteen-year-old nephew Sanford Clark into coming with him on a trip to Regina, the Saskatchewan province's capital. Sanford's parents agreed to let him go with his uncle. However, after the trip began, Gordon informed his nephew that they were not going to Regina. Instead, they were actually going to go to Los Angeles. After Sanford received some coaching from his uncle, the border crossing went without a hitch. Gordon had gotten Sanford into the United States illegally, and they were able to continue on to Southern California.

The pair stopped at George and Louise's house in Los Angeles before going on to the chicken ranch in Wineville. Later, Sanford testified that it was while they were staying with his grandparents that his uncle first molested him. Gordon continued to molest Sanford at least twice a week for the next two years.

Gordon and Sanford left Los Angeles about a week later and traveled out to the Northcott's Wineville property. At first, they slept in a tent while clearing the property of weeds and building the improvements. George, a trained carpenter, would come out from Los Angeles to help build the small four-room, wood-framed house. Over the next two years, other buildings were added to the property, including a garage, six chicken coops, a brooder house, chicken runs, a goat house, rabbit hutches and a small building to store grain.

This is the small, four-room house that Gordon Northcott, along with his father, George, and his nephew Sanford Clark, built on the property George purchased in Wineville. The photo was taken circa September 1928, after it was discovered that horrible crimes had been committed on the property. *Courtesy Riverside Metropolitan Museum.*

One might think that a twenty-one-year-old man who was kidnapping and molesting young boys would keep a low profile at his chicken ranch so as not to attract the attention of his neighbors. But that was not Gordon Northcott's style. He was known in the Wineville and West Riverside areas as a man of "peculiar characteristics." Gordon was a quarrelsome person who swore out complaints against several people in petty justice court while residing in Wineville. He even managed to obtain a search warrant for a nearby ranch based on his allegations that tires and other things he said were missing from his property would be found there. However, a search of the ranch by local law enforcement did not turn up anything, and officers dropped the case. Gordon also had a suit filed against him by a local man who claimed that Gordon had sold him spoiled chicken feed.

Starting in late summer 1926, Sanford found himself in a peculiar kind of hell with his uncle on the ranch in Wineville. Sanford was forced to do most of the work on the ranch, which included feeding and watering the animals and cleaning up after them, as well as cooking for Gordon. Sanford never knew what might set off his uncle's terrible temper, which would result in a beating with anything Gordon was able to lay his hands on. Occasionally, about ten or twelve times, as Sanford later testified, Gordon left the ranch in search of a young boy to molest. The boy would be brought to the ranch, blindfolded, and Gordon would send Sanford out of the house while he had his way with the new boy. An hour or two later, Gordon would take the boy away and release him. For over a year, this was Gordon's modus operandi.

Something changed on February 1, 1928. Gordon returned to the ranch and told Sanford that he had murdered a young Mexican man. Gordon had the man's severed head in a bucket, which he showed Sanford. The headless body had been dumped by the side of a road in Puente, where it was discovered the following day. Gordon made up an elaborate story about the killing and forced Sanford to memorize it. It had to do with hiring the young man to do work on the farm and the fellow threatening Gordon with a knife, forcing Gordon to shoot and kill the man in self-defense. Actually, the more truthful statement is probably the one that Gordon said later—that the man "knew too much." Sanford later testified that the Mexican man was never on the Wineville property and was not killed there. Unfortunately, the young man known as the "headless Mexican" in the press was never identified.

On March 10, nine-year-old Walter Collins disappeared from his home in the Lincoln Heights area of Los Angeles. Walter and his mother were customers in a grocery store where Gordon Northcutt had been employed for a short period of time, and it is thought that Walter met Northcutt there. Northcott kidnapped Walter and took him to the Wineville property. Instead of keeping Walter for just an hour or two, Gordon kept Walter locked up in a chicken coop on the ranch for about a week. Then Northcott got a call from his mother who told him she was coming out to the ranch that day. Louise arrived and, suspicious of what her son was hiding in the chicken coop, went out and found Walter Collins imprisoned there.

Louise was quite perturbed with her son, as little Walter knew Gordon and could identify him to police. She insisted that the problem be dealt with. In order to prevent anyone from going to the police, she forced both Gordon and her grandson Sanford to participate in the killing. She thought that none of the three could go to the police because incriminating the others would incriminate themselves just as much. Each took a turn hitting Walter in the head with the blunt end of an ax. He was buried in a grave dug inside one of the chicken coops.

Two months later, at about 10:00 p.m. on May 16, Gordon showed up at the ranch with Lewis and Nelson Winslow. The boys, twelve and ten, respectively, had been picked up near their home in Pomona as they walked home at about 8:30 p.m. from a Model Yacht Club meeting. Lewis had a book he had checked out from the Pomona Library with him that night. Gordon imprisoned the boys in one of the chicken coops on the ranch for about a week. Sanford was forced to bring them food and water and empty their chamber pot.

On or around May 25, Gordon announced to Sanford that it was time to kill the brothers. After an unsuccessful attempt to use ether to kill one of the boys, Lewis and Nelson were each struck over the head with the blunt side of an ax head, the same ax used to kill Walter Collins. Gordon struck the first blow on both boys but forced to Sanford to once again participate in the murders so that he wouldn't go to police. Obviously, Gordon had learned that lesson from his mother very well. Gordon also threatened Sanford that if he did not participate, Gordon would kill him as well. In spite of multiple blows from both Gordon and Sanford, both boys were still alive when they were placed in a grave and buried, again in one of the chicken coops.

The demented life Gordon had created at the Wineville ranch began to come apart in August. During the two years that Sanford was his uncle's captive, Gordon made him write letters home full of lies about going to school, having friends and the wonderful life he was living in Wineville. Jessie, Sanford's nineteen-year-old sister, became suspicious that her younger brother was not going to school because her brother's letters did not improve in grammar, spelling and composition over the two years that he had lived with his uncle. We don't know if she shared her suspicions with her mother, but in any case, it was young Jessie who made the trip to California to check up on Sanford. Jessie later said that she had been saving money to make a trip to California, having always wanted to see the state, particularly after Sanford moved there. She would find that neither her uncle nor her grandmother were particularly happy to see her.

Jessie came by ship down the coast, sending a telegram ahead announcing the time of her arrival. When no one was there at the dock to meet her, she made her way to a hotel, where she looked through a phone book and found the phone number of the hospital where her grandmother worked. Louise told her to stay at the hotel, and Gordon would come to get her. Gordon finally appeared the next morning and reluctantly took her to the Wineville ranch. Sanford was very happy to see his older sister, but Jessie was not pleased by what she saw. She could tell by Sanford's hands that he was working very hard, and she felt he looked thin and pale. She wanted to talk to Sanford, but Gordon never left them alone.

On the second night of her visit to the Wineville ranch, Jessie took matters into her own hands. After Jessie heard Gordon fall asleep, she snuck over to Sanford's bed, crawled in beside him and pulled the covers up over their heads to muffle the sound of their whispers. Jessie began asking her younger brother questions and finally got the full story of the lack of schooling, the beatings and the molestation. Sanford told her he was too afraid to try to get away and explained about the murders that had happened on the ranch.

After a week in what must have seemed like a house of horrors, Jessie went to Los Angeles to stay the rest of her visit at her grandparents' house. During those two weeks, she plotted and schemed to get her brother away from their uncle. She managed to help Sanford escape while they were at the Los Angeles house. During the few days he was hidden away, Gordon and Louise became very concerned. One day, they put a load of firewood in Gordon's car and drove off to the Wineville ranch. When Jessie asked her grandfather what they were doing he flat out told her they were going to get rid of evidence. Apparently Louise and Gordon wanted George to go with them, but he declined to help them with "their dirty work." It was during this trip to the ranch that Gordon and his mother dug up the three bodies of the boys that had been buried in the chicken coops. The wood was probably to be used to burn the bodies. While some bits of evidence were later found at the ranch, Gordon and his mother never told where they had disposed of what was left of the boys' bodies.

Sanford had been moved from his first hiding place to stay with a family that was friends of his grandfather. Unfortunately, after Gordon and Louise came back from the ranch, Gordon was in a tizzy. The next morning, he began arguing with George, scuffling with him, calling him names and threatening him with a gun. He began to threaten Jessie as well, and she ran out of the house. While she hid at the home of a neighbor who had befriended her, George admitted where Sanford was, and Gordon went and got him and took him back to the ranch.

Jessie, defeated in her efforts to get her brother away from the horrors of living with their uncle, returned to Canada in the middle of August. Gordon, realizing that the jig was probably up, began selling off everything he could at the Wineville ranch. Meanwhile, Jessie, upon her return to Canada, went to the American Counsel in Vancouver and swore out a statement that Sanford had been smuggled into the United States illegally, that he was being mistreated and that his life was in danger.

On August 30, the Los Angeles police department received a telegram from Canada asking them to find Gordon and investigate the accusation that he had smuggled Sanford into the United States illegally. They went to the Los Angeles house of George and Louise, spoke to them and made a report to the Immigration Service. The next day, August 31, two immigration inspectors arrived at the ranch around 11:00 a.m. Gordon saw them coming and ran off across the farm fields of Wineville. The inspectors searched the area for about two hours for Gordon and then gave up and took Sanford with them to Los Angeles.

After approximately two days in custody at the juvenile hall in Los Angeles, Sanford to begin to tell the story of his uncle and the Wineville ranch. On September 14, several police officers came to question Sanford. He told officers what had transpired out at the chicken ranch during the two years he had been there. When they heard about the murder of Walter Collins, they didn't know what to believe, as it had been a big news story. They put thirty photos of young boys on a table and asked Sanford to pick out the photo of the boy that had been murdered at the ranch. He picked the photo of little Walter. The officers then took Sanford out to the ranch, and as they searched the place, they found two rectangular holes in the floors of two of the chicken coops that had lime in them, as well as a cap that was soon identified by the father of the Winslow boys as little Nelson's. Needless to say, the police were beginning to believe Sanford's story of the horrors that went on at the ranch.

On the evening of September 14, Riverside County sheriff Clem Sweeters was called into the case by the Los Angeles detectives. He and

Sanford Clark, Gordon Northcott's nephew, is with two San Bernardino County sheriff's deputies at a property in that county that was being investigated as part of the infamous chicken coop murder case. *Courtesy Steve Lech.*

three of his deputies went out to the property that same evening to discuss the situation with their colleagues from Los Angeles. A guard was placed at the ranch and would remain in place, twenty-four hours a day, until Northcott's trial was over.

The Riverside County Sheriff's Department began conducting a thorough search of the ranch the following day. This search continued for months and found evidence of the crimes committed there including axes with human blood on them, numerous small human bones, finger nails and toenails, a tooth, two five-foot-deep graves that were empty but smelled strongly of the bodies that had recently been removed from them, pieces of human skulls and a board with a drawing of a yacht in blue and red crayon.

George Northcott was arrested and held as a material witness soon after the gruesome finds were made at the Wineville ranch. He was sixty-two years old at the time, and authorities were still trying to determine if he had any part in the crimes. He was never charged with any part of the murders, even though authorities acknowledged that, at the very least, he knew of the murders after the fact.

Meanwhile, on September 1, the day after Sanford was taken into custody, Gordon, with the help of his father, fled to Vancouver, Canada. His mother followed him a few days later. They enlisted the help of Gordon's sister Winnifred, and she joined her fugitive mother and brother for at least part of their life on the lam. On September 18, mother and son finally went their separate ways. Louise boarded a train for Calgary, while Gordon took a train to a seaport town and boarded the steamship *Sicamous*.

Even when in his best interests, Gordon still found it impossible to keep a low profile. On the ship, he demanded a stateroom even though he was just taking a daytrip, and he paid for his trip with a one-hundred-dollar American bill. These actions caught the attention of the purser on the ship. Once the purser took a good look at Gordon, he realized that the man in front of him looked like the description of the fugitive that was all over the newspapers.

After the ship docked, the authorities were called, and an officer followed Gordon onto the train he was taking, which happened to be heading back to the United States. The officer sat down next to Gordon and accused him of being a wanted fugitive. Gordon at first denied this, but eventually admitted his identity. He was returned to Vancouver the following day.

Louise was captured the same day because, just like her son, she insisted on bringing attention to herself. At the Calgary train station, she tried to buy a train ticket with a fifty-dollar American bill. Due to the fuss she put up while buying her ticket, the ticket agent paid more attention to her than usual. He then realized that she looked like the description he had heard on the radio the night before. She was arrested by police while on the transcontinental train that she had boarded in Calgary.

Riverside County authorities thought they would have their man, and his mother, back in their custody in a short amount of time. However, mistakes in paperwork and the decision by Gordon and Louise to fight their deportation prevented them from being returned. It was two months before Gordon returned to Southern California. Louise didn't follow

Gordon Stewart Northcott, circa 1928, during the time that he was fighting his extradition from Canada to the United States to face charges concerning the murder of young boys at his ranch in the Wineville area. *Courtesy Steve Lech.*

until a few weeks after her son. The Criminal Barrister, who was retained by Northcott in Canada to help him avoid extradition said, "If it is not disrespectful for me to speak of a client in this way, I thought he was a nut."

As soon as Gordon returned to Riverside County, he began playing games with law enforcement officials. He held out promises that he would take them to the burial places of Walter Collins and the Winslow brothers. Instead, these jaunts would turn into daylong or multiple day wild-goose chases that turned out to be a waste of time. Gordon never actually gave up the information that he had promised.

On December 10, two days after arriving back in Riverside County, Louise sent a note to Deputy District Attorney Earl Redwine asking to speak to him. Approximately a week later, Redwine met with Louise. She told him that George was not Gordon's father. Gordon was, in fact, the child of an English lord. Later, during Gordon's trail, she would claim that she put out this story to protect her daughter because, she claimed, Gordon was actually the result of an incestuous relationship between George and their daughter Winnifred. Gordon's father denied this claim, and there was never any proof that this was true.

Desperate to save her son in spite of the horrible acts he had committed, on December 29, Louise confessed to all of the crimes of which Gordon was accused. Deputy DA Redwine was not impressed with her made-up stories of murder. The following day, when she asked to see him again and once again wanted to confess, Redwine was not interested in hearing her relate another tale made up in some sick recess of her mind. Louise was told to make any confession in writing. She wrote out a brief confession admitting to killing Walter Collins by herself at the Wineville ranch.

The following day, Louise appeared before a judge and pled guilty to Walter Collins's murder. The judge sentenced her to life in the state prison. Louise escaped hanging, said the judge, only because she was a woman. Louise did her best to try and protect her son, but in the end, she only prevented him from being tried for Walter Collins's murder. He was still facing three other counts (for the Winslow brothers and the body that was never identified, known in the papers as the "headless Mexican").

Gordon's trial finally began on January 10, 1929, before an all-male jury. His arrogance continued throughout the trial. His lawyer did a heroic job of defending the undefensible, but he could not succeed in the face of the extreme arrogance of his client. Gordon made it known through his attorney that he wished to conduct the cross-examination of Sanford Clark, Jessie Clark and his father, George Northcott, himself. Then Gordon announced that he wished, from that moment forward, to take over his defense himself, without the benefit of his attorney. Reading about the behavior of Gordon during his trial, it is hard to remember that he was only twenty-two years old at the time.

On Friday, February 7, the jury began deliberating at 5:05 p.m. Even with a break for dinner, they were done with their deliberations at about 8:15 p.m. In spite of Gordon's efforts on his own behalf, it took the jury approximately two hours to find him guilty of killing the three boys. The following Monday, Gordon was given the death sentence and was soon transferred to San Quentin, where he took up residence on death row.

Of course, Gordon appealed his sentence. He contended in his appeal that the number and variety of trial errors entitled him to a new and impartial trial. His appeal went all the way to the California State Supreme Court. That court ruled on June 26, 1930, upholding Gordon's conviction for murder. On Wednesday, July 30, he was resentenced to hang on October 2.

While on death row, Gordon asked the governor of California, C.C. Young, for a pardon from the death sentence because he wanted to go out and preach the message of Jesus Christ to the world. Larry Newgent, a Los Angeles evangelist, claimed to have converted Gordon and tried to speak to the governor on Northcott's behalf. This ploy was unsuccessful.

Like a cat with a mouse, Gordon played with law enforcement, prison officials and the parents of his victims until the very last minute. He would say that he was going to tell them where the bodies of his victims were buried and then either deny that he had knowledge or tell them the bodies were in a spot on the chicken ranch that had already been dug repeatedly. In a move that was unprecedented, the prison warden allowed both Christine Collins, mother of Walter Collins, and Mrs. Nelson Winslow, mother of Louis and Nelson Winslow, individual audiences with Gordon in his cell on death row. However, both women were disappointed and left the cell weeping because he didn't give them any new information.

It appears that Gordon thought that a last minute reprieve would occur as long as he still held the information as to where the bodies were finally discarded. However, this game would no longer work. On October 2, 1930, as his death by hanging approached, Gordon Stewart Northcott fell apart. He required six guards to assist him up the steps to the gallows and two to stand with him as he waited for the trapdoor to fall. All the while, he pleaded, "Please don't, please don't!" Finally, at 10:10 a.m. at San Quentin State Prison, while his mother languished nearby in the women's section of the prison, Gordon's short, horrible life was finished.

Gordon's father, George Northcott, left California in 1931. He bought a small farm on the other side of the country in Parsonsburg, Maryland. In spite of all that came out before and during the trials of Louise and Gordon, George started a letter-writing campaign to get his wife paroled. Louise was paroled on May 30, 1940, after serving almost twelve years of her life sentence. She had been, apparently, a model prisoner. She arrived at her husband's farm in Maryland six days later.

Continuing the family tradition of not being satisfied with the status quo, Louise began almost immediately to ask for clemency. She argued that she should receive clemency because of her age (seventy-one) and the alleged mismanagement of her case at the hands of Sheriff Clem Sweeters and Deputy District Attorney Earl Redwine. However, in spite of her and her husband's efforts, the state parole board denied her request for a commutation of her sentence and recommended that she remain as a parolee. George died in April 1944, at the age of seventy-seven. Louise died just seven months later, in November of that same year. Their property and all of their belongings were left to their only surviving child, their daughter Winnifred.

Many people wonder what happened to Sanford Clark, the nephew who was beaten and abused but whose testimony was so important in convicting Gordon Northcutt. Sanford was made a ward of the State of California, and in February 1929, he entered the State Industrial School for Boys in Whittier. He was released in January 1931 and deported back to Canada. He married there in 1935. He and his wife never had children of their own, but they adopted two boys. He served honorably in World War II and then went on to have a career in the Canadian postal service. He rarely spoke of his ordeal at the hands of his uncle and never gave an interview on the subject. He was loved by his family and respected by his community. He passed away in 1991.

Such a horrific set of crimes would attract significant attention any time and place they were committed. The fact that these crimes occurred in a rural place like Wineville seemed to particularly capture the media's attention. A review of the *Los Angeles Times* archives found over 160 stories related to this case. It was reported in detail day after day throughout the country. While this was probably not the only reason why the community of Wineville decided to change its name, it was certainly one of the contributing factors. In 1931, Wineville became Mira Loma, the name by which it is still known today. One of the main roads in the area, and the road on which Gordon Northcott's house stands to this day, is still known as Wineville Road.

The information for this story was gleaned from the *Los Angeles Times*, the *Riverside Daily Press* and the *Riverside* Enterprise and from the book *Nothing is Strange with You* by James Jeffery Paul. Complete information on sources can be found in the bibliography at the end of this book.

Chapter 2

Wineville Lived Up to Its Name During Prohibition

Wineville, named for the wineries that sprung up in the rich sandy soil of the Cucamonga Valley, certainly lived up to its name during Prohibition. Prohibition lasted from 1920 to 1933 and made manufacturing and transporting of alcohol, other than for personal use, illegal. Needless to say, this was not a very popular constitutional amendment among much of the American public. With all of the previously legal distilleries forced to close, Prohibition gave rise to a huge underground market in liquor production and sales. Bootlegging, as it was known, was very profitable and helped make certain famous criminals, such as Al Capone, very rich.

We will probably never know how much bootlegging actually went on in Wineville, but newspaper stories from that time show that the illegal distilling of spirits was certainly active in that area. Bootleggers were getting caught, sometimes more than once. At that time, Wineville was an ideal place to set up illegal distilleries. It was a fairly isolated and sparsely populated farming community, located seven miles from both Riverside and Ontario. In spite of its remoteness, Wineville was located on a well-traveled highway between Los Angeles and Riverside. This made it an easy place to get to for the purchase of a few pints or a few gallons. It was also a convenient place to move ingredients into and product out of to the surrounding cities, especially Los Angeles. Wineville's proximity to Los Angeles was very important because Los Angeles was one of the wettest cities in the nation during Prohibition.

The Cucamonga Valley, which stretched from Wineville on its southeastern edge to today's city of Ontario to the northwest, was first planted with grapes in 1838, and by 1917, it was advertised as having five thousand acres of vineyards. These mature vines were probably supplying the bootleggers in the area with much of the raw product they needed to make various beverages, such as wine and brandy. Wineville was also home to experienced winemakers, many of them from Italy, who had the knowledge and the ingredients to make wine, but whose livelihood had been taken away by Prohibition.

In May 1921, the *Los Angeles Times* reported that "the largest still to be found since Prohibition began" had been discovered in full operation in Wineville. The still had the ability to produce about ten gallons of brandy a day. It was found half buried under the projecting roof of a henhouse. Several barrels of "excellent high proof brandy" were found buried in a barn and in other places on the property. You have to wonder how the newspaper knew that the brandy was of such excellent quality!

An early postcard of a grape vineyard in the Cucamonga Valley. *Courtesy Steve Lech.*

In February 1922, a raid on the A. Filippi house by county authorities found 2,750 gallons of red wine. Five officers conducted the raid and arrested the owner of the house, as well as G. Rumi, also of Wineville, and J.F. Graham, of West Riverside. The well-appointed winery was located in the basement of the home and included two 500-gallon wine vats. The officers confiscated thirty-five 50-gallon barrels of wine. Graham had employed two men, who happened to be undercover officers, to haul wine to Redlands, which exposed the operation.

In July 1924, a raid was conducted in Wineville after secret agents made undercover liquor purchases. Mike Bortolon, twenty-eight years old; his wife, also twenty-eight; and his brother Charles Bortolon, thirty-five, were arrested after approximately one hundred gallons of liquor were found on the property. The Bortolons were making good use of the sandy soil found in Wineville by burying most of the liquor in two-quart glass bottles around their yard.

The Bortolon Ranch was again the scene of two more raids in February 1925. Officers first raided the ranch on February 17. They found four thousand gallons of wine and once again arrested Mike Bortolon and his brother Charles, as well as another man named Matt Beltzler. It was Mike's third arrest in a year on charges of sale, possession and manufacture of liquor. There was a skillfully hidden cellar under the house that held five ninety-gallon barrels of wine. A barn on the property held a four-thousand-gallon vat. In the house, law enforcement officers found more than twenty-five gallon bottles of wine. On Friday, February 20, Sheriff Clemons A. "Clem" Sweeters and Undersheriff Carl F. Rayburn returned to the Bortolon Ranch and found an underground tank about fifty yards from where the previous cache was found. This tank, about six by eight feet in size, held another five hundred gallons of wine. The officers found it by probing that sandy Wineville soil with a long sharp stick.

Mike Bortolon had other problems as well. On a previous occasion, Bortolon had offered Sheriff Sweeters money to look the other way. No bribery charge was made in that incident because there were no witnesses. However, when the raid was carried out on February 17, Bortolon made another offer of $500 to Deputy Paul Scott, but this time, the sheriff's department made sure there were witnesses. Bail was set in Bortolon's case at $5,000, or a $10,000 property bond. It was the highest bail set up to that point for a bootlegging case in Riverside County.

In July 1927, what the *Riverside Daily Press* called a "super still" was found near Etiwanda Boulevard in the Wineville District. The *Press* went on to say that "it was the largest and most complete outfit for the illicit manufacture of liquor ever found in Riverside County, with seven complete stills capable of producing 1,500 gallons a day." The still was located by Riverside County deputy sheriff Paul Scott, who trailed cars bringing supplies from Los Angeles six different times before he finally located the operation.

Officers seized one hundred thousand gallons of mash, one hundred gallons of alcohol and seven stills and other liquor-making apparatus, valued at over $20,000. An elaborate system of alarms was set up around the ranch house and outbuildings, including a high water tower where a lookout could push buttons that rang gongs to give notice that the police were approaching. The raid was a success because the lookouts had left their posts to "pay a visit to the still room," said the *Los Angeles Times*. Eight federal prohibition agents and deputy sheriffs participated in the raid. They arrested Sam Mazzola, thirty-eight, of the Casa Blanca area of Riverside; Mimi DeGeorge, twenty, of Corona; and Frank Danieri Jr. of Wineville, also twenty. All three ended up being sentenced to three months in jail and each was required to pay a $250 fine.

The *Riverside Daily Press* reported in February 1928 that a Wineville rancher was arrested for bootlegging. The rancher was accused of selling wine and whiskey for $35 to $50 dollars a gallon. The rancher was held in the county jail after operatives from the sheriff's office made a purchase of liquor at the ranch using marked bills. Officers destroyed about one hundred gallons of liquor at the ranch. It was believed that more liquor and a still were still hidden on the property. The rancher later pled guilty and was fined $500, a substantial sum of money in 1928.

People of all ages took advantage of the times to make some money. A headline in the August 3, 1928 *Los Angeles Times* said, "Baby Bootleg Venders Taken." Apparently two teenage boys, Carl Vivonia, fifteen, and Reginald Devado, also fifteen, were pulled over by police. It turned out that they were in Vivonia's mother's car, which they had taken without permission. In the car were ten pint bottles of liquor. The boys said they found the liquor in a car in Los Angeles and decided steal it and drive to Wineville. At Wineville, they got jobs at the local cannery and began selling the liquor. One of the boys took officers to the location of their sales activities. There they found a gallon jug of liquor. Obviously, Wineville had a reputation by this point if the boys thought to go there to sell the liquor they found.

In December 1928, another still, once again declared to be one of the largest ever found in Southern California, was found in the Wineville area, just a half mile from the infamous Northcott house, where the Wineville Chicken Coop Murders occurred. In addition to the still, officers confiscated twenty thousand gallons of mash and hundreds of five-gallon cans. The cans were to be used to transport the 160-proof product to Southern California markets. It was estimated that the still and its accessories were worth $20,000. The product it could produce was obviously worth much more. The large liquor-making plant was located in the old adobe ranch house on the property. Three smaller stills were found under a pile of hay in the adjacent barn.

As time went on, the liquor manufacturing operations became more and more sophisticated. On September 13, 1931, federal prohibition officers raided the Montelepre Ranch near Wineville. They found a huge still hidden in a man-made underground cave that measured 250 feet by 25 feet. The entrance to the cave was hidden by several tons of hay. Officers had to tear away the hay to find the entrance to the underground room. Inside, they discovered 36,500 gallons of mash, a one-ton steam boiler, 125 sacks of sugar and two cars. Four men were arrested at the scene, one after he tried to escape out a secret rear passage.

The end of Prohibition in 1933 brought back many wineries to the Cucamonga Valley, including the Wineville area. By the mid-1940s, there were fifty-one wineries in the area with over thirty-five thousand acres planted in vineyards. It was the largest wine-producing area in the United States at that time.

Chapter 3

Belltown Murders Shocked Community

Summer in Southern California can last far into autumn. September 22, 1921, was just such a hot autumn day with a temperature that reached ninety-six degrees by early afternoon. That day, Chatham E. Helm Jr. and his son, Martin, drove to the sheriff's department in downtown Riverside to file a complaint against two men who they said had stolen hay from the Helm's ranch on North Main Street in Riverside. They told the sheriff that their hay was at a house in the unincorporated community of Belltown, which was across the Santa Ana River from Riverside.

Belltown traces its roots to 1907, when N.R. Bell subdivided land just north of the Santa Ana River in the West Riverside area. The subdivision, which Bell named for himself, consisted of just twelve lots, the majority of which were square, two-and-a-half-acre parcels. Considering the size of the lots, Bell was probably planning on marketing them to farmers who could grow truck crops or raise rabbits, chickens or other commodities that didn't require a large amount of land. Bell apparently wasn't very successful at selling these lots because seven years later, in June 1914, an amended subdivision map was filed by Bell and two partners, which resubdivided all but lots 1, 10 and 12 of the original plan. The new subdivision had sixty-nine lots, all rectangular in shape, all approximately 75 feet wide by 150 feet deep.

According to the 1920 census, Belltown, or the "Bell Tract," as it was called in the census, had about thirty-four households and 180 people.

Quite probably more people lived there and just weren't recorded by the census taker. It was still a very rural area without shops, businesses, paved roads or other features of a more built-up community. It did have a one-room elementary school from 1912 until 1918, when the school was closed. The school did not reopen until 1925. The first church was not built in Belltown until 1927.

Belltown was primarily populated by Mexican immigrant families. Many of the men worked at the nearby cement plant in Crestmore. Others were day laborers at area farms or orange groves. They tended to speak Spanish, at least according to the census. Six English-speaking families also lived in Belltown at that time, as well as one household headed by Italian immigrants and another headed by Japanese immigrants.

Chatham. E. Helm Jr., the man who reported his hay missing, and his family lived in Pomona but had a ranch they also farmed in Riverside. They had bought the land in Riverside from A.A. Rouse less than a year before. Chatham and his wife, Susie, had three children. Their oldest, Martin, was born in 1904, daughter Ivy was born in 1908 and their youngest daughter, Dorothy, was born in 1914. The Helm family had moved around some in pursuit of making a living farming. In 1910, the family was living in Valley Center in San Diego County. By January 1920, the Helm family was living in Imperial County. The family then moved to Pomona, where their son Martin attended Pomona High School. Martin was finishing up the summer's work on the Helm's Riverside ranch on September 22 and planning to return to school the following Monday.

The alfalfa hay the Helms were raising on their Riverside ranch was a very common money crop in those days. Some of the hay was fed to the animals on the ranch or farm where it was grown. The rest was sold as a cash crop. Alfalfa was a very successful crop in Southern California. In most parts of the world, it is cut and harvested four times a year. But in Southern California, it can be harvested up to twelve times a year. California is still a leading alfalfa-growing state.

Because Belltown was in an unincorporated area, the Riverside County Sheriff's Department provided law enforcement. The sheriff's department was located in the county seat of Riverside, at the corner of Eleventh and Orange Streets, in a building that also housed the county

Frank P. Wilson, Riverside County sheriff from 1907–23. *Courtesy Steve Lech.*

jail. After Chatham and Martin reported the hay theft, Sheriff Frank Wilson assigned Deputy Sheriff Henry Nelson and Reserve Deputy Sheriff Theodore Crossley to go to Belltown and try to round up the suspects in the theft. It was agreed that Martin would go along to identify the men he and his father said had stolen the hay.

Reserve Deputy Theodore Crossley was a businessman in the city of Riverside. He owned an automobile repair garage and sales showroom where he sold Mitchell Touring Cars. Born in New York City in 1877, Crossley's parents were from England and were in the United States temporarily for his father's work. The Crossley family returned to England, and Crossley was raised there in the city of Manchester. His father passed away when he was just eight years old. At the age of ten, he was sent to learn the trade of toolmaker and die sinker. His mother died when he was sixteen, and a year later, Theodore returned to the country of his birth. He was able to go into business for himself in New York City by the time he was twenty-one. It was apparently love at first sight when he saw his first automobile, and Crossley became known as an automobile enthusiast and was considered an excellent driver.

After a fire destroyed Crossley's business in New York City in 1904, he wasn't quite sure what to do with his life. He happened to see a sign advertising train travel with "cheap rates to California." That made up his mind, and off he went. After the long desert crossing, he got off at the first city he saw—San Bernardino. Crossley bought a bicycle and traveled all over Southern California, visiting various cities before deciding to settle in Riverside. There he opened the Orange Valley Garage and

Deputy Theodore Crossley. *Courtesy Riverside County Sheriff's Department.*

Theodore Crossley's garage. *Courtesy Steve Lech.*

gradually built up his business in repairing and servicing automobiles and eventually began selling them as well. On June 6, 1917, he married widow Idella Webb. She had two sons, Elvin and John.

Crossley had made himself and his cars available to the sheriff's department for many years, and he later joined the sheriff's department as a special deputy. His skill as a driver and his fast cars, the last one a six-cylinder Mitchell sedan, made him a valuable member of the department, and he provided transportation for deputies when he was called on to do so. He was frequently called on for special assignments.

Deputy Henry Fredrick Nelson was born in 1874 in Andover, Illinois, to Swedish immigrants. Andover was the site of the first Swedish Lutheran Church in the United States and had been a destination for Swedish immigrants since 1849. Nelson moved to California in 1891 with his brother George. They took up ranching, and Henry continued ranching for another five years after he moved to Riverside in 1894. He purchased an orange grove in Riverside in 1899 or 1900, which he later sold. He married Anna S. Ringburg on August 6, 1902, in Riverside. She also had Swedish immigrant parents and had also been born in Illinois, so the two

Deputy Sheriff Henry Nelson. *Courtesy Riverside County Sheriff's Department.*

had much in common. Henry and Anna had three children—a boy born in 1904, a girl born in 1906 and another boy born in 1911.

Nelson joined the Riverside County Sheriff's Department on January 7, 1907, as one of only two deputies appointed during Sheriff Wilson's first term. For many years, he served as jailer at the county jail in downtown Riverside. He, along with his wife and children, resided on the second floor of the jail. By 1920, Anna was acting as the matron at the jail as well. Deputy Nelson was one of the most popular officers on Sheriff Wilson's staff.

The Helms had accused Juan Palmarin and Vincente Melgosa,* both reportedly twenty-five years old, of stealing their hay. It just so happened that Palmarin had been a recent inmate at the county jail. About five weeks before the hay was stolen, the sheriff's department conducted an early morning raid on the Palmarin house on C Street in Belltown. Deputy Nelson was the officer that made Palmarin get out of bed that morning. Crossley also participated in the raid, and Palmarin was taken to the county jail in Crossley's car. He and other members of his family

* Vincente Melgosa was later identified as Luis Guillen. For the purposes of this story, he will be identified by the first name he was reported under.

were arrested for bootlegging and having Indian hemp or "loco weed" (marijuana) in their possession. It was believed that the incident that unfolded on September 22 was due to a grudge held against the deputies.

According to Chatham Helm, he had gone to the Palmarin house the morning of September 22 to retrieve the hay stolen from his property. He was accompanied by his son Martin and by C.E. Weaver. While talking to Juan Palmarin about the hay, Juan's mother, Lina Palmarin, had gone into the house, and when she came out, she handed Juan a revolver. After that encounter, Chatham went to the sheriff's station to report the theft.

Henry Nelson is shown standing in front of the Riverside County Sheriff's Department in downtown Riverside. *Courtesy Steve Lech.*

Deputy Crossley, age forty-four, drove Deputy Nelson, forty-six, and Martin Helm in his car to Belltown to look for the thieves. Nelson was in the front passenger seat, and Martin was in the back. For unknown reasons, the *Riverside Daily Press* later identified the area as Bellville, and that mistake was picked up by the *Los Angeles Times* and has been perpetuated in print and on the Internet ever since. However, based on the description of where the crime occurred and the fact that no local history books can be found that refer to a Bellville, it's certain that the shooting occurred in Belltown.

When the deputies and Martin Helm arrived in Belltown, they drove down C Street, where Martin saw and identified Palmarin and Melgosa. Crossley stopped the car, and Nelson told the men, "I want you boys." Nelson got out of the car with a pair of handcuffs and started to put them on one of the men. That man broke free just as the other man pulled a gun, reportedly an automatic revolver, and shot Nelson in the chest.

Crossley saw what was happening and reportedly called out "Watch out, Henry!" but it was too late. Crossley began to get out of his car, but the man with the gun turned and shot Crossley, who fell out of the car. Martin was shot in the back as he tried to hide in the back seat of the car. The shooters ran in the direction of the river bottom as one of them was heard to shout in Spanish, "Let's get out of here!"

Neighbors who heard the shots came to their aid. Mary Grillo, the fourteen-year-old daughter of Emilio and Amelia Grillo, Italian immigrants who owned property at the corner of Fourth Street (now Twenty-fourth Street) and C Street (now Hall Avenue), heard the shots and went out to the road to see what had happened. She saw the bodies of the two deputies and a bleeding Martin Helm leaning over the body of Deputy Nelson. She helped Martin to her porch and gave him some water and then went to call the sheriff. When she came back out, she went to Deputy Crossley, who was crying out faintly for help. She tried to talk to him, but he did not respond. She then went to Nelson and tried to talk to him, but he only stared at her.

Leonard C. Williams, a rancher who also lived nearby, heard the shots as well. He saw two men running toward the river bottom. One was dressed in blue overalls and the other in khaki pants and a blue coat. He also went to the scene of the shooting. There he found Crossley dead and Nelson under the front of the car. He assisted Nelson to his feet, but Nelson was unable to stand and slumped to the ground, where he leaned on his hand.

G.R. Wilson was in the front room of his house in Belltown when he heard the shooting. He looked out his front window and saw Nelson and Crossley on the ground and Martin Helm just getting out of the car. He also saw a man in blue overalls running away, but otherwise could not identify him.

By the time help arrived, Crossley was dead. Nelson and Helm were rushed to Riverside Community Hospital. Nelson died there an hour and a half later. Martin was in critical condition and not expected to live.

Within an hour of the killings, posses were formed by the sheriff to hunt for the suspects. Fifty men responded to the call that afternoon, and the number swelled to 250 by nightfall. Posses were formed in San Bernardino to begin searching the river bottom in that county. Two army airplanes from March Field were used to search for the fugitives from the air. Searchlights were brought in that evening from March and were placed on bridges and other high points to flood the river area with light. There was even talk of putting floodlights on top of Mount Rubidoux, but it was decided that they wouldn't have been strong enough to do any good.

The reward for the capture of the two men quickly swelled to $1,500, a great sum in 1921. The *Daily Press* put out a special edition at 7:00 p.m. on the evening of the murders. The news of the deaths of the two deputies who were also well-known community members shocked the city of Riverside and the surrounding communities.

The manhunt continued for days. However, in spite of visiting every Mexican settlement in western Riverside County and supposedly searching every house in those settlements, the fugitives were nowhere to be found. By September 28, a local newspaper lamented, "The two men have disappeared as though the earth had opened and swallowed them up."

On October 14, 1921, almost three weeks after the murder of the two deputies, a car carrying six people, three men and three women, was stopped in Indio by a United States revenue officer. When Officer Fred H. Schwartz approached the car, he recognized two of the men as suspects in the slaying of the two deputies. As Schwartz played his flashlight around the interior of the car, he saw suspect Vincente Melgosa in the act of drawing a revolver. Schwartz managed to beat Melgosa to the draw. Juan Palmarin immediately jumped from the car. The officer fired four times at the fleeing suspect but did not hit him. The officer ordered the rest of the people out of the car before allowing Melgosa to exit. He then marched the three women, the driver of the car and the suspect to the Indio jail. Melgosa had to be subdued with a blow to the head in order to be placed behind bars.

Within a day or two, Melgosa was taken to the Los Angeles County Jail. It was decided not to bring him to the Riverside County Jail due to the "feeling that exists here," according to the October 18 edition of the *Los Angeles Times*. Meanwhile, a posse continued to search for Juan Palmarin. On October 17, Melgosa was brought to West Riverside, where he was given a preliminary hearing before Justice Briggs of the West Riverside Township Justice Court. He was charged with first-degree murder.

Melgosa was also taken to Riverside Community Hospital where, according to the *Times*, "he was confronted by Martin Helm, the seventeen-year-old boy who has survived the shot fired into his body… Helm identified the prisoner as the man who did the shooting." It should be noted that Helm had previously said that he believed Juan Palmarin was the shooter. It appears that Melgosa was kept at the San Bernardino County Jail after this point, primarily to keep him separate from Reyes Floriana, the driver of the car in which he was found, and from Juan Palmarin's father, both of whom were in the small Riverside County Jail.

The justice system in 1921 moved much more quickly than it does today. Jury selection for Melgosa's trial began on November 22. Justice Freeman, the presiding judge in the case, appointed attorney C.H. Benshoof to represent Melgosa. Benshoof requested three times the usual number of potential jurors be called for the jury selection. Fifty men from all over western Riverside County were summoned to Riverside for the jury selection. The selection was finalized that same afternoon.

The trial of Melgosa started on the morning of November 23. Martin Helm, the primary witness to the case, was still hospitalized, and so, in order to hear his testimony, the court and jury adjourned to Riverside Community Hospital later that day. There, Helm identified Melgosa as the shooter and identified the man's gun and sombrero as well.

The trial lasted just two days. The jury began deliberations late in the afternoon on November 25. A verdict of guilty was reached at 5:06 p.m. after a deliberation of just 56 minutes. On November 30, Judge Freeman sentenced Melgosa to death by hanging. At the sentencing, Melgosa said, "I am not guilty. You can sentence me." The prisoner was immediately sent to San Quentin, where the hanging would take place. Melgosa's sentence was carried out on February 24, 1922. He was just the fourth man to be given the death sentence since Riverside County had formed in 1893.

Meanwhile, Riverside County sheriff Frank Wilson received a letter from the Mexican counsel at Los Angeles saying that the counsel had received a letter signed by thirty-nine Mexican residents of San Bernardino charging that Melgosa had been treated with "great cruelty" while he was imprisoned in the San Bernardino and Riverside County Jails. Sheriff Wilson denied the charge. The case received extensive coverage in area Spanish-language newspapers.

Martin Helm spent five months in Riverside Community Hospital. He was finally able to return to his home in Pomona on February 18, 1922. He had not been expected to live, due to the gunshot wound and the infection that followed. Unfortunately, Martin Helm never fully recovered from his gunshot wounds. He continued to be in and out of the hospital for the next year and finally died on February 11, 1923. In January 1924, his parents filed a suit against the Riverside County Sheriff's Department with the State Industrial Accident Commission. In their claim for damages, they alleged that Helm, who was seventeen at the time of the shooting, was deputized by Sheriff Wilson through his deputies and given a shotgun but no shells.

Juan Palmarin, the other suspect, remained at large. He was seen in Mexico several times by local police officers, but efforts to bring him back to the United States for trial were never successful.

Idella Webb Crossley, Theodore Crossley's widow, continued living in Riverside and did not remarry. Her two sons, Elvin and John Webb, took over the running of Crossley Garage and Auto Sales after Theodore

Theodore Crossley's headstone in Evergreen Cemetery, Riverside. *Courtesy Christine Brooks Ericson.*

Henry Nelson's headstone in Evergreen Cemetery, Riverside. *Courtesy Christine Brooks Ericson.*

Crossley's death. Idella passed away in 1933 and was buried near her husband in Evergreen Cemetery.

Anna Nelson and her children had to find a new home after their husband and father was killed because they lived above the jail. His murder not only stole him from their lives but also took away the only home the children had ever known. Anna moved her family to a home at 393 West Fourteenth Street. By 1925, she had opened a grocery store on Lime Street, and her oldest son, Sidney, worked for her. By 1930, Sidney was married, had one child and had taken over as proprietor of the grocery store his mother started. Anna's youngest son, Henry, was working as a florist in Los Angeles in 1930. Daughter Evelyn began working for a local doctor and, by 1931, was a nurse with Walker, Miller and Miller. Anna passed away in 1970 at the age of ninety-three. She never remarried.

Chapter 4

Poison Gas Spill Could Have Been a Tragedy

There was a cyanide gas leak on January 6, 1928, that affected a number of people but, amazingly, killed no one. The newspaper accounts were confusing, but a few bits of information are certain. A drum of cyanide fell off a vehicle driven by a man whose first initial was J. and whose last name was Black. A number of people were affected, in addition to the driver. The accident that caused the leak happened in the West Riverside district. But beyond these pieces of information, the two Riverside newspapers, the *Riverside Enterprise* and the *Riverside Daily Press*, had two widely divergent stories concerning an incident that could have turned into a terrible tragedy.

First, before we delve into this mystery of conflicting reporting any further, let's explore why Mr. J. Black was driving around with cyanide in the first place. Beginning in the early part of the twentieth century, cyanide was used for the fumigation of orange groves to eliminate scale insects on the citrus trees. It was also used to fumigate houses to rid them of pests, primarily bedbugs. The same cyanide that was used in the gas chambers on death row to kill convicted criminals was just as effective at killing bugs. The cyanide was usually transported to the job site in metal barrels or drums.

When cyanide was used in citrus groves, the trees were covered with tents, and the gas was pumped under the tent. The tenting was done at night, as the cyanide caused damage to the trees if used during the heat

The Standard Cyclopedia of Horticulture, published in 1914, includes this drawing showing how citrus trees were tented for cyanide fumigation.

of the day. When it was used in the groves, the poisonous gas wafted out from under the tents and into the surrounding neighborhoods, occasionally knocking out or even killing animals or people.

Even at very low levels of exposure, cyanide causes people to pass out. Sometimes the grove workers who were gassing the trees would lose consciousness from accidentally inhaling the gas. They would be moved away from the tented trees so that they could get fresh air, and when they woke up, they usually went back to work. Occasionally, workers were killed by overexposure to the cyanide gas. It is amazing it didn't happen more often.

The man driving the vehicle with the cyanide was reported as J.R. Black by the *Enterprise* and J.H. Black by the *Press*. According to the *Press*, Black had his two young sons with him. The *Enterprise* reported that he had one young son named Charles with him. Both papers agreed that at about four o'clock in the afternoon on Friday January 6, 1928, Black was driving a vehicle for the Charles Baisel Fumigating Company on Mission Boulevard, just past the Union Pacific railroad tracks, near today's intersection of Van Buren Boulevard and Etiwanda Avenue. The *Press* said that Black was driving a sedan with a one-hundred-gallon drum of cyanide strapped to the front bumper. This seems improbable, as typical drums hold fifty-five gallons, and even that would be impossibly large to strap to a sedan's front bumper. The *Enterprise* said that he was driving a truck, and the drum of poisonous cyanide was in the bed of the truck. That seems much more likely.

What the *Enterprise* Said

According to the *Enterprise*, Black was driving a truck and with him was his small son Charles. In the bed of the truck was a drum of cyanide gas. Black was near his own service station, and as he made a turn onto the highway, the drum fell from the truck onto the pavement and began leaking the deadly gas. Black followed the safety protocol of the day and threw a lighted match on the gas to burn it up. There was a concern that his son Charles had been injured by the gas. Thankfully, he was not injured and was put to bed that night, according to the *Enterprise*, "none the worse for the wear." The *Enterprise* reported that the quick action of Black prevented any gas from escaping into the surrounding area. No other persons were reported as being affected. The *Enterprise* did not explain why, if Black had a service station, he was also working for the Baisel Fumigating Company.

What the *Press* Said

The *Press* reported that a one-hundred-gallon drum of cyanide was strapped to the bumper of Black's sedan. In the back seat of the car were Black's two young sons. According to the *Press*, the drum of deadly gas came loose when Black, attempting to pass another car, ran a front wheel off the pavement and jarred the drum loose from its moorings. The drum became lodged under the car and was dragged for a number of feet, finally coming free in front of a service station owned by J.H. Fisher. Black began to be affected by the leaking gas but was able to drag his small sons to a nearby field, where he began trying to revive the

This gas station was located at the corner of Mission Boulevard and Wallace Street, circa 1930. It is typical of gas stations in the Jurupa Valley area at that time. *Courtesy Marjorie Page.*

Riverside City Hospital, later known as Riverside Community Hospital. *Courtesy Steve Lech.*

younger one, who had passed out as a result of the gas. The *Press* said the mishap had happened near another service station owned by Augustus C. "Clyde" Ertel, age thirty-nine. Although there was a considerable distance separating the gas container from the station, fumes drifted through the air and rendered Ertel; his wife Carrie, thirty-eight; and four-year-old son Ronald unconscious. The Ertels also had a two-year-old daughter named Esther, but she was not mentioned in the newspaper articles. Their older daughters, Eileen, age thirteen, and Leota, nine, were in school at the time of the accident. When the fumes dissipated, Clyde Ertel regained consciousness and rushed his family to Riverside Community Hospital for emergency treatment.

Meanwhile, Sunnyslope area residents William and Hattie Nogle, both forty-seven, were in their own car, approaching the site where the drum of gas had crashed to the ground a few minutes before. Mrs. Nogle later reported that they saw a discolored spot on the pavement of the road but just assumed that some gasoline had spilled there. They didn't realize the danger that lingered in the air and continued driving toward the scene of the accident on Mission Boulevard. When they reached the discolored pavement, the cyanide gas seeped into the Nogles's car, and Mr. Nogle began to lose consciousness, causing their car to crash into a ditch at the side of the road. Mrs. Nogle was only half conscious herself, and as she tried to get out of the car, she fell to the ground. She was able to get back up and did her best to administer first aid to her husband. They both then managed to stagger to Ertel's service station in search of help.

Mrs. Nogle was quoted in the *Riverside Daily Press* as saying, "It was the most terrible experience I ever went through. Just as we struck that gas patch everything seemed to go black. I couldn't breathe. It seemed as though a dark curtain had been pulled over my eyes, and the first thing I sensed was the feeling that I was going to die."

The *Enterprise* called Mrs. Charles Baisel, who lived in West Riverside. She said that the Baisel Fumigating Company realized the dangerous character of the cyanide gas they carried. In the ten to twelve years that her company had been in business, she stated, about fifteen people had been killed by cyanide gas accidents in California, while at the same time hundreds of people were employed in the industry. This, she indicated, was a small number compared to the number of people killed in traffic accidents during the same time period.

It seems to have been pure luck that no one was killed in the aftermath of the accident and cyanide gas release. It was noted in the *Riverside Daily Press* that Sherriff Clem Sweeters planned to launch a thorough investigation into the transportation of poisonous cyanide on public highways. Less than two weeks later, the County Board of Supervisors instructed the district attorney to create a new ordinance regulating the transport of deadly substances such as cyanide and dynamite on county highways. This was a direct result of the accident on January 6.

No further information could be found on truck driver J.H. or J.R. Black and his young sons. Clyde Ertel lived fifteen more years and passed away in 1945. His wife, Carrie, lived until 1964. Young Ronald Ertel, who was rushed to the hospital by his father, went on to serve in World War II and passed away in 1973. Little Esther, who was probably affected by the gas although she was not mentioned in the newspapers, grew up and married, but passed away at the young age of twenty-five in 1951. William Nogle was a bookkeeper for a local gravel quarry at the time of the accident. He lived until 1955, passing away when he was sixty-four years old. His wife, Hattie, lived to be ninety-two and passed away in 1973.

Chapter 5

Shooting Mishap or Murder?

Hilda Throop, age twenty-five, was shot to death on Wednesday, September 13, 1916, at her in-laws' home in Glen Avon. That is the one fact that we know is true. But was it an accident, as her husband Charles insisted? Or was it murder for insurance money, as the Western Indemnity Insurance Company claimed?

Only a little is known about the lives of Charles and Hilda Throop prior to Hilda's death. Charles Bailey Throop and Hilda E. Anderson were both born in California. Charles was one of five children. Hilda may have been the child of immigrant parents, as an acquaintance said that Charles had referred to her as "a big Swede." They married in 1912, possibly at the suggestion of Charles's father. She was twenty-two and he was twenty-one at the time.

After their marriage, Charles and Hilda went to Illinois. There, in about 1913, their only child, a daughter, was born. By 1916, the Throops had returned to live in Los Angeles, California. Charles's parents, Richard and Mary Throop, owned an adobe house on about twenty-six acres in the community of Glen Avon. Their property was located just east of Agate Street on the north side of Corundum Street and was referred to as the "Throop Ranch" in a local paper. Charles and Hilda and their small daughter had come to visit Charles's parents on Saturday, September 9.

According to Charles and his sister Hazel Headrick, who was also present in the house the day of the incident, Charles was making plans to go out shooting. He had laid out three guns in the enclosed porch at the rear of the house. Hilda told him he couldn't go until he did the dishes. Charles was on the porch. Hilda entered and, according to Charles, "playfully" grabbed the gun in Charles's hands. Hazel, who was in another room of the house, testified that she heard Hilda laughing just as the gun went off. The bullet went into Hilda's chest near her heart and killed her almost instantly. Charles said he caught her as she fell and that she died with "a smile on her face." The county coroner determined that the shooting was an accident.

However, the Western Indemnity Insurance Company was suspicious. Charles Throop had taken out two accidental death policies amounting to $13,000 just weeks before Hilda's death. The insurance company sent investigator T.W. Haas to the Throops' home. He reported that the clothes that Hilda had been wearing had already been burned by the family, and her corset, showing a hole in an area near the heart, was in the boiler being washed. The insurance company refused to pay out on the insurance policies. Charles Throop filed suit to obtain the money from the policies. The sensational superior court trial was reported in local papers during February and March 1918.

The insurance company lawyer brought forth dramatic testimony from a witness who cast suspicion on Charles's story. Fred L. Sexton, an elderly friend, testified that he and Charles had a conversation about a year before the tragic shooting. Charles said then that there were problems in his marriage and asked how much it cost to get a divorce. When Mr. Sexton asked if there was someone else, Charles told him of a young girl he had known for a number of years that was "his kind." He told Sexton that if he could get a divorce, the girl's mother would be willing for them to marry.

The *Los Angeles Times* was not afraid to print some of the racier testimony. Mr. Sexton testified that Charles Throop said "when he put his arms around the girl and laid his hands on her breast it was like the sweet perfume of flowers." Mr. Sexton thought Charles called the girl Beulah. Charles married a girl named Beulah Bowers in 1917, about a year after his wife's death. She was eight years younger than him, which would have made her sixteen years old at the time of Hilda's shooting.

Charles had told the police that he was holding a sixteen-gauge shotgun, which was the gun that Hilda had grabbed and which inflicted the fatal wound. On the third day of the trial, he changed his testimony about the type of gun that was in his hands on that September day. Charles said it was actually an eleven-gauge shotgun that he had been holding. This was very important because the sixteen-gauge gun could not have accidentally gone off while the gun was cocked and so could not have fired accidentally when Hilda grabbed it.

The court found the case in favor of the insurance company. It declared that Hilda Throop's death was the result of gross negligence on the part of Charles Throop, who did not exercise ordinary care or caution in the handling of the shotgun that killed Hilda. The court also said that Hilda was not in any way responsible for her injuries. Because of these findings, Mr. Throop was denied the money from the accidental death policies he had taken out on his wife.

Charles Throop decided to appeal the superior court decision. On September 20, 1920, the state appeals court ruled on Throop versus Western Indemnity Company. It found that the bodily injuries suffered by Hilda were sustained in a manner that fell within the terms of the insurance policies. The court said that the fact that the discharge of the gun was due to the gross negligence of Mr. Throop excluded the possibility that the plaintiff intentionally shot the victim, and therefore the shooting was accidental. The policies taken out on Mrs. Throop were for accidental death, and she died in a manner that was accidental, the court ruled. Therefore, Mr. Throop was due the money from the insurance policies. The insurance company further appealed the case to the state supreme court, but on November 18, 1920, it was denied a hearing. Charles Throop had finally won the accidental death insurance money from the death of his wife Hilda.

It is hard to fathom why Charles Throop fought so hard and so long for $13,000. He would have had to spend a considerable amount of money on attorney's fees to take his case all the way to the state appeals court. Trying to determine the worth of money in 1916 dollars compared to today's dollars is not simple. There are many different ways to calculate it. Depending on the method used, that $13,000 is equivalent to anywhere from $280,000 to $3.8 million in 2012 dollars. Perhaps it wasn't the money. Charles Throop may have just wanted to clear his name.

Did Charles Throop kill his first wife, Hilda? It seems very odd that Charles would take out accidental death insurance on his wife. There is no evidence that she worked outside the home, and in that day and time, she was more likely to die from disease or childbirth than an accident. At the same time, it seems unlikely that Charles could have planned the shooting as it ended up happening. Perhaps it was a crime of convenience, an opportunity taken by a man unhappy in his marriage. It seems plausible that Charles, seizing the chance to shoot Hilda, was then immediately struck by horror and remorse and began straightaway to claim that the incident was an accident. We do know that he lived for many years after the accident and was never again accused of a violent crime. We will never know for certain if Hilda Throop's death, in an adobe house in Glen Avon, was an accident or not.

After her death, Hilda Throop was taken almost immediately to a Los Angeles–area funeral home. A notice was printed the day after her death in the *Riverside Enterprise* advising that her funeral would be held September 16 in Los Angeles. She was likely buried in a cemetery in that city. By 1920, her father- and mother-in-law were living with their daughter Hazel and her family in Los Angeles. Hilda's little daughter was six years old and living with them. Both Richard and Mary Throop lived until 1951, when they died five months apart in South Pasadena, California. Charles and Hilda's daughter married in 1940. She had at least one child. No other information could be found for her.

What happened to Charles Throop? By June 5, 1917, when he registered for the draft, he listed himself as a widower who was an apartment housekeeper living at 344 South Olive Street in Los Angeles. Charles married Beulah Bower, the young woman who was mentioned during the court case, in the later part of 1917. They had one child, a daughter, in December 1918. Charles and Beulah later divorced, and Charles married for the third time in 1934. His new wife, Doreen Hoover, was eighteen years younger than her husband. They went on to have three children together. In the 1920 census, Charles Throop was listed as a real estate agent, and by 1930, he had become a real estate broker, a career he seems to have had for the rest of his working life. He died in Marin County, California, in 1987.

Chapter 6

Blind Pig Blamed for Murder

How can a blind pig cause a murder? The term "blind pig" refers to a low-class establishment that sells liquor illegally. Camps full of laborers were prime locations for blind pigs to become established. However, lots of men who are away from their families and working very hard every day combined with illegal alcohol sales rarely results in a good outcome. Such was the case on the night of July 28, 1909, when Pedro Rodriguez shot Jesus Espinosa and Octaviano Aguerre.

The crime occurred at the California Construction Company's Bly Camp. The camp, located in the Pyrite Canyon area, lodged the Mexican laborers who worked at the Bly Brothers quarry in the east fork of Pyrite Canyon. In 1909, the mining operation was leased by the California Construction Company from the Bly Brothers Stone Company, although the quarry was still known by the Bly Brothers name.

Mining began in the Pyrite Canyon area about 1900, when the West Riverside Granite Company started the first quarry there. Soon thereafter, there were two quarries in Pyrite Canyon that were worked by the Bly Brothers. By 1906, the Bly Brothers owned three hundred acres in Pyrite Canyon and were working five separate mines on the property. Stone from the two quarries was shipped to the Bly Brothers stone yard at Seventh and Alameda in Los Angeles for cutting and finishing.

Stone from those quarries was used in 1903 on the facade of the Hellman Building in Los Angeles. That project required fifty train carloads, or

Mission Boulevard stretches out through West Riverside (now Rubidoux) toward Glen Avon in this 1920s-era photo taken from Mount Rubidoux. To the right in the distance are the hills where Pyrite Canyon and the Bly Brothers quarries were located. *Courtesy Riverside Metropolitan Museum*

This is a particularly large dimension stone being hauled from the quarries in Pyrite Canyon by a team of twenty mules and horses. *Courtesy Riverside Metropolitan Museum.*

The Hellman Building in Los Angeles used granite from Pyrite Canyon on its façade. *Courtesy author.*

ten thousand square feet, of Pyrite Canyon stone. The *Los Angeles Times* reported that the stone from the Bly Brothers quarry near Riverside was "light-gray granite of exquisite beauty." The Hellman Building, now known as Blanco Popular, is still located at the northeast corner of South Spring and Fourth Streets, in the Spring Street Financial District area of downtown Los Angeles. It has been recognized as a city of Los Angeles cultural landmark. The building has been converted into lofts.

At the time of the shooting, the Bly Brothers quarry was an important source of stone for the San Pedro Breakwater, which was completed in

1911. It was estimated that the quarries in Pyrite Canyon contributed 125,000 tons of granite blocks for that project. The breakwater project required about two hundred men to work the quarries and produce the fifteen or more train carloads of granite block per day that was shipped out to San Pedro.

On Wednesday night, July 28, five men gathered in Pedro Rodriguez's shack near the quarry to drink. They included Rodriguez, Espinosa and Aguerre, as well as two men identified in a local newspaper as R. Rodriguez and J. Barasa. During an interview with Sheriff Wilson and Deputy Sheriff Evans the next day, Espinosa was able to tell them that he had been drinking and had bought liquor from Rodriguez. A subsequent search of Rodriguez's shack unearthed a large quantity of beer.

In later testimony and interviews, Rodriguez gave his side of the story. He admitted that he had a stock of beer that he was selling to Aguerre and Espinosa. A quarrel started after the two men ran out of money but attempted to get more beer from Rodriguez.

At his preliminary hearing on August 3, Rodriguez added more information through his testimony. Rodriguez said through an interpreter that he had a supply of liquor in his house and that Espinosa and Aguerre had been drinking with him earlier in the evening. The two men left and when they came back, Espinosa came at him with a knife because Rodriguez refused to give him any more liquor. Rodriguez further testified that after the shooting he went directly to wake up the foreman of the camp and dropped the gun along the way. According to what was printed in the August 4 edition of the *Riverside Enterprise*, Rodriguez said, "I have nothing more to say than I did this in my own defense. Espinosa entered my house with a knife in his hand and was going to cut me."

According to local newspapers, Rodriguez shot the two men through a gap in the doorframe of his house. Espinosa received bullet wounds to the abdomen, behind the left knee and through the left arm below the elbow. Aguerre received a flesh wound from a bullet in his side. After being shot, Espinosa and Aguerre tried to get to the quarry bunkhouse, which was located about two hundred yards from Rodriguez's place. However, they were not able to make it, and both fell to the ground. Rodriguez ran to the residence of the quarry foreman to tell him of the incident, later saying that he dropped the gun as he ran.

Quarry foreman Oscar Dowling was awakened by Rodriguez. Dowling called the sheriff immediately. Shortly thereafter, Sheriff Frank Wilson, Deputies Henry Nelson and Wallace Evans and coroner Dr. Charles Dickson arrived at the scene. According to the Riverside newspaper the *Morning Mission*, they were taken to the camp "in a high power automobile driven by Ted Crossley." Crossley was a reserve deputy and the owner of an auto dealership in Riverside. He was well known for his skill as a driver, so it isn't surprising that the sheriff called on Crossley and his car to get him and his men to the scene of the murder quickly from the sheriff's office in downtown Riverside.

When the officers and doctor arrived at the scene, they determined that Espinosa was in very serious condition and not expected to live through the night. They decided to make him comfortable at Bly Camp and not to move him that night. Aguerre was examined and found to have just a flesh wound in his side. Dr. Dickson removed the bullet and dressed the wound, and then Aguerre was transported to the county jail to be held as a material witness.

Rodriguez was questioned by Deputy Sheriff Nelson and at first refused to admit to firing the shots that struck the two men. Deputy Nelson conducted a thorough search of the area and finally found the revolver that had been used in the shooting buried in the dirt near where Espinosa had fallen after staggering away from the scene of the shooting. All of its chambers were empty. At that point, Rodriguez broke down and admitted to shooting Espinosa and Aguerre.

Espinosa managed to live through the night, so the next morning, he was transported by ambulance to County Hospital, which was located at that time in the Arlington area of Riverside, at Magnolia Avenue and Harrison Street. At the hospital, it was decided to perform a risky operation as a last ditch attempt to save his life. Five doctors were in attendance to participate in the surgery. However, as Espinosa was being wheeled to the operating room, it became obvious that he was breathing his last. He died that afternoon at about 4:30 p.m.

An inquest into Espinosa's death was held the following day. The coroner's jury selected to hear the findings in the inquest consisted of O.W. Johnson, S.M. Guthrie, Swan Johnson, S.S. Coakley, C.E. Alden and W.L. Wilburn. The jury determined that Espinosa died from the abdominal wound he received and that he must have been facing Rodriguez when the fatal shot was fired. They held Rodriguez responsible for Espinosa's death and found that he acted without justification.

Rodriguez was arraigned on August 7 in superior court. The court appointed Hugh H. Craig as his attorney. Craig asked for a two-week delay in which to plea to the charge, and that request was granted. A local newspaper reported that Sheriff Wilson had been trying to persuade Rodriguez to enter a guilty plea on a manslaughter charge. Rodriguez apparently finally agreed to do so, and on August 28, he did plead guilty to manslaughter. At the time, the maximum sentence for this charge was ten years. His attorney asked for judicial leniency in the matter. In view of the fact that the defendant pleaded guilty and saved the court the expense of a trial, three years were taken off his sentence and Rodriquez was sentenced to seven years.

Sheriff Wilson, with the assistance of a man named Archie Mills, left to take Rodriguez to San Quentin the very next day. Octaviano Aguerre, the other man shot by Rodriguez, had been recovering from his wound in the county jail, where he was being held as a witness. When Rodriguez pled guilty on August 28, Aguerre was finally released that day as well.

Chapter 7

Cold Weather May Have Clouded Their Judgment

Levi Montgomery and his wife, Eliza, married in Minnesota in about 1869, and they spent the next thirty years there as farmers, including a number of years on their 160-acre farm near the tiny town of Monroe, in the southwestern part of that state. During that time, the Montgomerys endured not just the usual cold snowy weather of the upper Midwest, but also some of the most extraordinary winters on record. They survived what is known as the "Little Ice Age," six years of abnormally cold and damaging weather that lasted from the winter of 1882–83 to the winter of 1887–88. Then, after a decade of more normal cold and snow, they had to deal with the "winter that almost wasn't." The winter of 1898–99 was unusually mild, particularly in the upper Midwest. It was mild, that is, until January 30, 1899. Beginning on the second to last day of January and lasting until the middle of February, much of the country experienced a cold snap of epic proportions. In that short period of time, the entire length of the Mississippi River froze and ice flowed into the Gulf of Mexico. A snowfall record was set in Washington D.C. that was not broken until 2010. Virtually the entire United States was battered by the most remarkable set of cold waves in the history of the Weather Bureau.

It is no surprise that, having endured such horrible weather, the advertisement that C.S. McLaury placed in a Minnesota newspaper caught the eye of Levi Montgomery. In late 1898 or early 1899, McLaury advertised his desire to trade a thirty-five-acre property that included an orange grove at Glen Avon, California, for a Minnesota farm. Imagine what Levi, fifty-two, and Eliza, fifty, must have talked about: farming in an area where it never snows, having a place where you could grow crops year-round, owning a grove of orange trees and, in the dead of winter, picking a ripe orange off a tree in your yard. Levi Montgomery saw the ad that promised a very different life, and he responded to it. His correspondence with McLaury resulted in the Montgomerys trading their Minnesota farm, which included a mortgage of $2,000, for the property in the Glen Avon area, sight unseen, with a note for an additional $4,000. The deal was consummated on February 28, 1899, just two weeks after the "Great Cold Wave" swept over Minnesota.

Levi and Eliza Montgomery had seven children: George, Ida May, Robert, Ernest, Harry, Clayton and Ralph. Only the two youngest were still at home when the Montgomerys packed up to move to their new property in Southern California, "land of sunshine."

The new property was located on the southwest corner of Corundum (now Mission Boulevard) and Agate Streets. It included a small house that, in 1899, was worth just thirty dollars. When the Montgomery family arrived in Glen Avon in 1899, they found a rural community that consisted of small and large farms and a one-room school that was only four years old at the time. Their land was located on the main street in the Glen Avon area, although it was still a dirt road at that time. The community of West Riverside, with its few stores, was a fifteen-minute wagon ride away. Another fifteen minutes past West Riverside was Riverside, the county seat and largest town in Riverside County. At the center of the navel orange–growing region of Southern California, Riverside had stores, banks, churches, trolley lines and an opera house.

Unfortunately, the Montgomerys did not find the paradise they were looking for. The thirty-five acres they took ownership of did not live up to the description they had received in their correspondence with McLaury. Levi was so disgusted with the property that he filed suit on January 13, 1900, to void the entire deal and to collect damages in the amount of $7,000. The law firm of Gibson and Gill from Riverside represented him.

The case was heard in the Superior Court of Riverside County, beginning over a year later on April 2, 1901. On that day, Levi took the

The Glen Avon School, a one-room schoolhouse, was built in 1895 on two acres of land located on Pyrite Street. *Courtesy Jurupa Unified School District.*

stand to testify. He said that McLaury represented to him that twenty acres of the thirty-five acre property were planted with bearing orange trees, six to eight years old; that ten acres were planted in younger trees that were not yet bearing; and that five acres were uncultivated. He further testified that he was told that the property had a perpetual water right; that the land needed no fertilizer; the soil was soft like a snow bank and looked like pounded brick, with a uniform depth of seventy-five feet; no hard winds ever blew, but about noon a soft breeze came up; and that there were one thousand boxes of oranges on the trees. He said he was also told that Magnolia Avenue ran to the land and that a streetcar line was within eighty rods (440 yards) of the property. Levi swore he had been swindled. He said the soil was gray and hardpan, that the orange trees only had 250 boxes of inferior fruit on them and that the land was not properly graded or flumed for irrigation. Today it is impossible to speak to the state of the orange trees on the property or how well the land was graded. However, anyone who has put shovel to dirt in the Glen Avon area knows that the soil in that area is not soft as a snow bank.

The dirt there is hard as a rock. Glen Avon, like the rest of Southern California, also experiences the epic winds known as Santa Anas that blow through the area, particularly in the winter.

On April 3, A.P. Robinson, A.J. Parks, W.B. Hunter, T. Brown and P.B. Stephenson, as well as others, testified that the Glen Avon property bought by the Montgomerys from McLaury was unsuitable for orange growing and that the trees on the land were of poor quality. It was asserted by some of the witnesses that the ground was so hard that the orange trees had to be planted in holes that were made with dynamite.

On April 4, C.S. McLaury had his opportunity to take the stand. He testified that he was a land agent based in Clinton, Iowa, and had never seen the land in West Riverside until he came out to answer the Montgomery's complaint. He denied that he had ever told the Montgomerys that the land was near Magnolia Avenue or that it had a $2,000 orange crop on it. While we are not privy to what information was given before the Montgomerys agreed to the property exchange, there is evidence that McLaury was not telling the complete truth concerning what he knew about the Glen Avon property. The March 34, 1899 edition of the *Riverside Daily Press*, published less than a month after the Montgomerys signed the documents for the exchange, reported that C.S. McLaury of Sheldon, Iowa, had been in Riverside for "some days." It was also mentioned that Mr. McLaury owned property adjacent to the city, most likely referring to the land in Glen Avon.

On June 5, Judge Noyes handed down a verdict in the case. The court decreed that the note for $4,000 was void and awarded the Montgomerys $1,800 in damages. In other words, the court believed that the Montgomerys had been cheated in the land exchange to the tune of $5,800.

At the end of July 1901, C.S. McLaury and his partners in the property appealed their loss in the Riverside County court to the California Supreme Court. The case was argued in front of the Supreme Court in April 1902 during one of their half yearly sessions in Los Angeles. It is not known why the case took so long to reach a conclusion but, finally, on April 25, 1904, the Montgomerys' long fight for justice was finished. The California Supreme Court upheld the lower court ruling canceling the $4,000 mortgage and ordering C.S. McLaury, J.L. McLaury and their wives to pay the Montgomerys

$1,800. The Montgomerys vacationed at Newport Beach in August of that year, possibly to celebrate their court win.

Unfortunately, this was not the only legal case Levi and Eliza Montgomery had to contend with. On June 19, 1901, William Smith filed suit to collect $4,000 on a mortgage of the Montgomerys'. In the original land exchange, the Montgomerys had exchanged 160 acres and a $2,000 mortgage for the thirty-five acres in Glen Avon and a $4,000 mortgage. This promissory note on the Glen Avon property was held by C.S. McLaury, his brother J.L. McLaury and their wives. The McLaurys had transferred the $4,000 note to William S. Smith on April 1, 1899. The suit by Smith was against both the Montgomerys and the McLaurys. Understandably, Smith was just trying to get his money back on the mortgage he had taken over from the McLaurys. After the Supreme Court ruled in 1904 that the $4,000 mortgage was null and void, the case brought by William Smith was dismissed. Finally, all of the legal issues related to the Glen Avon property were resolved.

In spite of the disappointment Levi experienced on seeing the new property in Glen Avon, this did not stop him from becoming a part of the community. In the important county courthouse bond election in July 1902, Levi was a ballot clerk in the Union voting district. He also acted as a deputy sheriff to prevent fruit thefts at West Riverside.

Unfortunately, at the same time the Montgomerys were fighting their court battle and settling in to their new community, Levi was experiencing problems with rheumatism. Rheumatism is an old-fashioned medical term that is no longer in use. At that time, it referred to pain in the joints, such as the pain from arthritis, or it referred to generalized pain and weakness, such as the type that might come from a heart condition. Apparently, Levi had a heart condition that, at the time, was virtually untreatable.

On the morning of May 3, 1906, Levi had refused to eat breakfast and later walked away from the ranch. His wife Eliza wasn't too concerned, as her husband had been acting peculiar recently. But when Levi did not return, she became alarmed. She asked her neighbors to help her search for her husband. A neighbor named Mr. Abbot discovered Levi's lifeless body lying in a field, not too far from the Montgomerys' house. Levi had pinned a note to his vest that read, "I have taken poison. No one is to blame. God have mercy on my wife and Ralph." A bottle of strychnine, used to kill gophers, was lying next to his body. His failing health had become too much to bear, apparently. He was sixty years old. Who knows how much the long, drawn-out court battles contributed to his health problems.

Eliza Montgomery never remarried. She split her time, living with her son Ralph or her son Clayton for the rest of her life. It was reported in the local newspaper that, for her seventieth birthday in 1918, Eliza was thrown a surprise birthday party. Her family and friends gave her a comfortable rocking chair. She was able to enjoy that rocking chair for another fifteen years. Eliza died in 1935, at the age of eighty-five, and was buried next to her husband at Evergreen Cemetery in Riverside.

Ralph married Edith Bennett in 1915 when he was twenty-one years old. He and his wife had one child, a daughter named Gertrude. By 1920, Ralph and his family had moved to San Bernardino, and Ralph had given up the ranching business to become a building contractor. He eventually became an electrician for the Kaiser Steel Company. He passed away in 1975 at the age of eighty.

Clayton, the other son that moved with his parents to Glen Avon, married Gladys Mangels of Riverside on June 4, 1921. They had four children, two boys and two girls. Clayton remained a farmer in the Glen Avon area. He died at the age of ninety-six in 1986.

Chapter 8

Blame the Brandy for Tragic Shooting

Back in the day, it always seemed to be the same question: Was a shooting on purpose or was it an accident? Law enforcement and the person who got shot usually claimed it was on purpose. The person holding the gun at the time of the shooting vigorously denied that claim and said it was an accident. Such was the case of the unfortunate shooting of Berenabe Balcebeas.* Balcebeas was shot on May 1, 1907. The person holding the gun at the time of the shooting was Jesus Chavez, a fact that even Chavez admitted was true.

Balcebeas, about thirty-three years of age and a native of Mexico, was a member of a crew that was employed by Rodgers Development Company to clean a ditch in the Stalder area, now known as Mira Loma. Balcebeas was considered a good worker and a quiet man. He said he was camping in a tent by himself near the Salt Lake railroad tracks on May 1 when the events that would end his life unfolded.

Jesus Chavez, fifty-two, was a resident of El Monte, a town located to the west, in Los Angeles County. It was believed that he had come to the area for the "Mexican celebration," according to a local newspaper. Given the date, the celebration referred to was presumably Cinco de Mayo. It was also believed that he was traveling from El Monte to Colton

* The names and spelling of the names of people of Mexican origin were often questionable in the local newspapers of the time. The victim was also said to be Veranze Mansibai. I was unable to find any information on either name from other sources.

These stone winery buildings at the Guasti Winery may have been where Chavez purchased his bottle of brandy. The buildings were erected in 1904. *Courtesy Steve Lech.*

when the shooting occurred. Chavez's mode of transportation was his spring wagon, pulled by a pair of horses, one white and one bay.

According to Chavez, as he was traveling through the Stalder area, he stopped at the Stalder Winery and purchased a bottle of brandy. He fully admitted that he became quite drunk and stayed that way for the duration of the events as they eventually unfolded. When contacted after Chavez's arrest, the Stalder Winery insisted that they never sold liquor to Mexicans, Italians or Indians. The person at the winery suggested that it was possible that the man got his booze at another winery that was located about two miles from Stalder (probably in the Guasti area).

Chavez said that as he was driving along the county road (later Mission Boulevard) in his rig, near the Salt Lake tracks in West Riverside, three or four men rushed toward him and his wagon. One of the men noticed Chavez's shotgun under the seat of the wagon because the barrel of the gun was visible. The unknown man may have even tried to snatch the gun. Chavez grabbed for the barrel of his gun in self-defense and said that the hammer snagged on something and the gun discharged, severely injuring two of his fingers. Other than his own injury, Chavez said he had no idea what had happened to the shot and that he left the area immediately.

Balcebeas was taken to the Riverside County Hospital, located in the Arlington area of Riverside. *Courtesy Steve Lech.*

Balcebeas received a glancing blow to his face with Chavez's shotgun. While it did not kill him, it did do extensive damage to his right eye and the right side of his face. Someone camped in the same area as Balcebeas supposedly started to walk to the nearby city of Riverside to get help for him. However, that person never arrived in Riverside, and Balcebeas was not picked up by ambulance and transported to the county hospital in Riverside until the following day around noon. In spite of his grievous injuries, Balcebeas was able to relate his version of events to his rescuers, to the sheriff and a sheriff's deputy and to hospital personnel. Unfortunately, due to the medical care that was, or was not, available in 1907, Balcebeas's condition deteriorated, and he died on Tuesday, May 7, at 4:00 p.m.

With no idea who did the shooting and with only descriptions of the shooter and his wagon and horses to go on, Constable John Baird and Deputy Henry Nelson spent the afternoon of May 2 scouring the Jurupa Valley area looking for the assailant, but no trace of his whereabouts could be found. On the morning of Saturday, May 4, Sheriff Frank Wilson and Deputy Wallace Evans went to Colton and, armed with the descriptions of the shooter's wagon and horses, located both. The two officers searched nearby dwellings until they found Chavez, and he was arrested without incident. When Balcebeas died three days later, the incident changed from a shooting to possible murder.

On May 8, the day after Balcebeas's demise, an inquest was held before a coroner's jury to determine the cause of the victim's death. The jury convened at Squire and Flagg's undertaking rooms, where the body had been taken. The local newspapers reported that the following men were on the jury: L.V.W. Brown, Eugene Smith, W.C. Moore, E.E. Wiggins, G.W. Hart and W.H. Burger.

Sheriff Wilson was the first witness to testify. He said that he had examined Chavez's wagon and there were shot marks on the side of the seat. Mrs. Eliza Montgomery, fifty-five, who lived on Corundum Street (now Mission Boulevard) in the Glen Avon area, testified that she met the victim on the road just after the shooting. She said that she did see one man running after Chavez's wagon. A local paper reported that someone by the name of Mumy, who was not further identified, examined the tent on the Monday after the shooting. He found Balcebeas's hat in the tent, and it was full of holes. This person was most likely Harvey Mumy, a resident of West Riverside.

Deputy Evans testified at the inquest that Balcebeas told him that Chavez had come by where he was camping and wanted him to drink with him. When Balcebeas refused Chavez's offer to drink, Balcebeas said that the man in the rig had shot him. O.A. Powell, superintendent of the hospital, testified that the injured man told him the same story as he told Deputy Evans. However, Evans also testified that at the hospital Balcebeas had changed his story and told Evans that he didn't know how the shooting occurred.

Interpreter M. D'Albar, who rode with the victim to Riverside in the ambulance and was with him at the hospital, testified that Balcebeas told him the same story during the ambulance ride as Deputy Evans had related. D'Albar testified that, later at the hospital, Balcebeas told him a different story. There, Balcebeas said that Chavez hit the gun on a bottle, and it accidentally discharged.

Constable Baird told of finding the victim in a tent. There were a number of bullet holes in the tent, and it was apparent that the victim was close to the wagon when he was shot. He further testified that it was apparent that the shot must have been fired from the wagon.

After the testimony, the coroner's jury reached the following verdict: "We, the jury, find that Berenabe Balcebeas came to his death by a gun in the possession of Jesus Chavez, May 1. We further recommend that the said Jesus Chavez be held pending further investigation. [Signed] L.V.W. Brown, Foreman."

Once the coroner's jury rendered their verdict, the local Riverside newspapers fell silent on this case. Had it progressed to a verdict and a trip to San Quentin for Jesus Chavez, it is likely the newspapers would have reported on it, as they did with so many other similar crimes of that time. However, if the case had quietly ground to a halt due to lack of evidence, then other stories may have garnered the attention of local reporters.

Chapter 9

Mrs. Cote Takes On the Power Company

It was 1914 and electric power was coming to Jurupa Valley. But in echoes of current-day battles over the placement of electric power poles, John C. Cote (pronounced Co-tee) and his wife, Grace, took on the Pacific Light and Power Company.

John and Grace Cote married about 1906 in Missouri when he was thirty and she was twenty-four. They soon had two children. Their son John E. Cote was born in 1907 and their daughter Alice was born in 1908. The Cotes moved to the Glen Avon area in 1911, where they purchased forty acres at the southeast corner of Agate and Corundum Streets. The property was vacant when they purchased it, but they quickly built a house on their land. The 1912 tax assessment fixed the value of the house at fifty dollars. John farmed their land and raised a variety of crops. Grace became involved in the community Sunday school and the Friendship club, both of which provided entertainment for the family.

As is still the case today, utility companies at that time had to enter into franchise agreements with local governments in order to be allowed to provide their services to residents. The Pacific Light and Power Company entered into just such a franchise agreement with the Riverside County Board of Supervisors. Board of Supervisors Ordinance 106 gave the power company a fifty-year right to construct, operate and maintain an electric pole and wire system for the purpose of distributing electricity

This view of Glen Avon, circa 1910, was taken from the hills above the community and looks south across the groves, farm fields and little houses that dotted the area at that time. *Courtesy Linda Spinney.*

along all public roads and highways in the county of Riverside, outside incorporated cities. The terms and conditions in the ordinance also required that the power company locate its poles in conformity with instructions from the County Board of Supervisors.

The Pacific Light and Power Company applied to the Board of Supervisors to be allowed to erect poles on Agate Street in the Glen Avon area. The poles, as required by the franchise agreement, were to be placed in the public street right of way. The property owners along Agate Street vehemently opposed this plan. They claimed that Agate Street was not a public street, and therefore, there was no public right of way in which to place the poles. The Board of Supervisors agreed that Agate Street had never been dedicated as a public street or highway and denied the application of the power company.

In late 1913, the power company sent a work crew to the Jurupa Valley area. According to the December 22 *Riverside Daily Press*, the Pacific Light and Power Company had a camp at the Montgomerys' property and "several men at work putting in their high line from the company's plant at Corona through this section." The Montgomerys lived across Agate Street from the Cotes. The power company appears to have used its crew to dig holes along Agate Street for power poles, including holes for four poles on the Cotes' property.

The Cotes and their neighbors were probably outraged at the arrogant attitude of the Power Company and ready for a fight. Soon after the holes were dug, a work crew of approximately twenty-five men appeared with heavy equipment, including a derrick, to place power poles into the holes. Mr. Cote was not home at that time, and Mrs. Cote, with five-year-old Alice and seven-year-old John at her side, confronted the work crew.

The work crew likely had no idea about the Agate Street property owners' dispute or the decision by the Board of Supervisors denying the power company the right to put poles along Agate Street. However, even if they did, the crew also had their orders to set poles and their jobs probably depended on them following orders.

When Mrs. Cote realized what was going on, she rushed to the west side of her property. She put little Alice in one hole and little John in another, and then she ran between the other two holes, doing her best to prevent the crew from setting power poles into the holes. Mrs. Cote was pretty successful for a while, too. The crew leader later admitted that Mrs. Cote prevented the crew from doing work for at least two hours.

The work crew probably thought they had a crazy woman on their hands. The crew moved the derrick back and forth a few times from hole to hole, trying to set a pole, but, as one crewmember later said, "Mrs. Cote was there all the time." C.R. Turner, timekeeper for the company, took a dozen snapshots of the battle while it was going on. Later, he said the camera was his and he took the pictures "purely for my own pleasure." When asked if Mrs. Cote objected to having her picture taken, Mr. Turner replied, "Yes, but many women object to having their pictures taken."

As the standoff dragged on, it attracted the attention of one of the Cotes' neighbors. Ralph Montgomery, who lived across Agate Street from the Cotes, said he saw one of the workmen push Mrs. Cote into a hole. Then one of the work crew, a man by the name of Frank Grathouse, lifted her away from the hole, but roughly, said Montgomery, and "in no gentlemanly manner." When Montgomery told the man to leave her alone, Montgomery was told to stay out of it or he would get his block knocked off.

Frank Grathouse, the same workman who pulled Mrs. Cote back out of the hole she was either pushed into or fell into, also tried to scare one of the children away by throwing lighted fuses into the hole their mother had placed them in. It is not known which child he tried to scare—Alice or John.

The Cotes filed a suit on January 5, 1914, against the Pacific Light and Power Company. In that suit, they sought to prevent that company from setting power poles on their property. Mrs. Cote also filed charges against a number of the workmen for assault and battery. District Attorney Lyman Evans agreed that she had been poorly treated and decided to prosecute a case against five of the workmen.

Mrs. Cote claimed that one of the workmen had shoved her into one of the power pole holes, badly bruising her arm and shoulder. According to the testimony of Fred. G. Durkies, the work crew's foreman, as reported in the *Riverside Enterprise*, "I did not see anybody shove Mrs. Cote into the hole. I told the men to be careful not to hurt the lady. Our work was delayed by her, but we finally got a pole into one of the holes. Mrs. Cote had hold of the pole all the time, was swinging on it, and the pole, being top heavy as it hung from the derrick, weaved back and forth and Mrs. Cote slipped into the hole. Mr. Grathouse grabbed her, not roughly, and helped her out of the hole."

On February 17, a headline in the *Riverside Enterprise* read "Court Approves Brave Defense of Property by Gritty Woman." In what the *Enterprise* described as "the most important decision reached in a local justice court in many months," Justice Ellis ruled that two employees of the Pacific Light and Power Company were guilty of assaulting Mrs. Cote. Fred Durkies, the crew foreman, was fined $25 and crewmember Frank Grathouse was fined $50. Judge Ellis dropped the charges against the other three crewmembers.

Judge Ellis ruled that no evidence was produced at the trial that showed that Agate Street was ever dedicated and accepted as a public road and, further, that no evidence was given that showed that Agate Street was used by the public as a street or highway. Therefore, said Ellis, the power company had no right to set poles on the Cote property or anywhere along Agate Street. Justice Ellis said, "I think the violence threatened and done to Mrs. Cote was beyond justification and contrary to law, that the acts perpetrated were wrong and unwarranted and Mrs. Cote in her attempted defense of what she believed her legal rights in defense of her property, displayed bravery and heroism rarely witnessed."

Three years later, in 1917, the Pacific Light and Power Company became part of Southern California Edison, the company that provides electricity to Jurupa Valley today. Grace Cote passed away in 1943 at the age of sixty-two. John C. Cote passed away in 1955 at the age of eighty-four. They are buried next to each other in Evergreen Cemetery in Riverside.

The 1930 census indicated that the then twenty-one-year-old Alice was still living with her parents and was, ironically, working as a bookkeeper for a power company. Alice and John both married and provided their parents with several grandchildren. John began working as a bookkeeper for a trucking company and worked his way up until he became the owner of Citizens Truck Company in Riverside. Both Alice and John had very long lives, living past their ninetieth birthdays. The entire Cote family remained in the Jurupa Valley and Riverside areas throughout their lives.

Chapter 10

Strange Murder-Suicide Case Shocks Glen Avon

The middle of July 1918, was a momentous time in the history of the world. On July 15, the French overwhelmed the Germans in the Second Battle of the Marne, which was the turning point of World War I. On July 17, on the order of the Bolshevik Party, the Russian czar and his family were executed. But for the residents of the rural community of Glen Avon, these major news events were overshadowed by the shocking deaths of Walter and Anna Baldwin on the evening of July 19. The sheriff and coroner determined that their deaths were a murder-suicide. But were they?

Walter and Anna came from very different worlds. Walter Baldwin was born in Iowa in 1885, and his family soon moved to San Bernardino, where his father worked for the railroad. The family lived in a middle-class neighborhood, and Walter was able to attend high school before he went out into the working world. Anna was born in Sweden in 1883. Tragically, her mother died just a week after she was born. Her father, with the help of his sister, raised Anna and her six siblings. At the age of seventeen, Anna moved to Stockholm to work as a maid. When she was twenty, Anna gave birth to a daughter she named Greta Elisabeth. Because the baby was born out of wedlock and Anna was a single mother, she was forced to place baby Greta with a foster family just a few months later.

It appears that Anna had a difficult time after she had to give up her baby. She moved around Sweden quite a bit, and in 1909, she entered into a short-lived marriage. Meanwhile, Anna's oldest sister, Olga, and her husband, Waldemar Konig, had immigrated to the Los Angeles area. There they settled down and opened a barbershop. Olga and Waldemar never had any children of their own, and in 1909, they sent for Anna's daughter Greta to come live with them. The little six-year-old girl traveled from Sweden to the United States with a young missionary couple. Other family members also moved from Sweden to the Los Angeles area, and in 1917, Anna decided to join her family in Southern California.

When Anna arrived in Los Angeles, she lived briefly with her sister Olga. Anna got to see her daughter Greta for the first time in nine years. That summer, Anna and Greta went to stay with another of Anna's sisters, Hildegard. Hildegard and a man named Karl Johnson were living together as man and wife, even though they never married, and they had one son together. Karl managed an orange grove in the inland Southern California area. After the summer break, Greta returned to her Aunt Olga's house. After all the years apart, she and her mother did not have a close relationship.

During the summer at Hildegard and Karl's ranch, if the family stories are true, Anna had an affair with her sister's "husband" Karl Johnson. Anna also met one of Karl's workers, thirty-two-year-old Walter Baldwin. By the end of the year, Anna married Walter. After they married, Walter and Anna moved to what is now Jurupa Valley. There they began farming a piece of land on Jurupa Road, near Pedley Road, in the Glen Avon area. The Baldwins lived in a small house on the property that they were farming. Their partners in this enterprise were Walter Baldwin's sister and brother-in-law, Maude and Walter Ross. The Rosses lived very close by, either on the same property or right next door. Maude was twenty-seven at that time, and her husband was twenty-six. They had one daughter who was five.

According to the story that has been passed down in Anna's family, the Rosses and Baldwins leased the Jurupa Valley farmland from the Slater brothers. One of the brothers came by to see how the harvest had gone and immediately became infatuated with the beautiful Anna Baldwin. Mr. Slater started coming by frequently to call on Anna when her husband was out in the fields. Anna must have told her sister Hildegard about the situation because Hildegard's "husband" Karl found out about the visits.

Pedley Road, looking north toward Jurupa Road, still looks today much like the country road it was in 1917 when the Baldwins would have used it. *Courtesy author.*

Anna's daughter Greta later told family members that Karl was very jealous of Anna's marriage to Walter Baldwin. Greta said that Karl went to Walter one day (we presume July 19) and told him about Mr. Slater's many visits, adding that he thought that Anna and Slater were having an affair. Greta believed that Karl was hoping he could break up the Baldwin's marriage, and he could have Anna back. The news enraged Walter. He came in from the fields, and he and Anna began quarreling about the supposed affair with Mr. Slater. Anna was furious at the accusation and told Walter she was leaving him.

A little after 7:00 p.m. on the night of July 19, just as the summer light was fading, Maude and Walter Ross reported that they could hear Anna and Walter quarreling. Maude told her husband to go over and see if he could smooth things over. As Walter Ross was walking toward the Baldwins' place, he heard the sound of a rifle shot and then another. Family members were later told that Anna had been walking across the yard from the laundry room, where she had been gathering her clothes to leave. As she crossed the yard, her husband emerged from their house and shot her twice. The local newspapers said that Walter Ross arrived just in time to see Anna as she staggered around one corner of the house and fell dead. The family story is that Walter Ross found Anna's husband, Walter Baldwin, on the ground cradling Anna. Baldwin told Ross to leave because he didn't want to have to hurt him, and then he put the short-barreled rifle he had just used to kill his wife against his own chest and pulled the trigger. The bullet struck Walter Baldwin in the left shoulder.

According to what Walter Ross later told the sheriff, he then wrestled the shotgun away from Walter Baldwin, who fell to the ground. Walter Ross assumed that Walter Baldwin was dying, but Baldwin got back onto his feet and rushed into the house. He found another rifle and shot himself twice more, once in the abdomen and once in the chest. Ross saw Baldwin fall to the ground, and once again, Ross thought Baldwin was done for, even dead. Ross ran back to his property and got in his automobile to drive to a nearby telephone to call the sheriff.

Meanwhile, if the events played out as Walter Ross later stated and as reported in the local newspapers, Walter Baldwin was not, in fact, dead. He was instead coming to the realization that he had killed his wife and that he, in spite of three gunshots, had not managed to kill himself. While Walter Ross was gone telephoning the sheriff, Walter Baldwin got back up, went into the house, found a barber's razor that had belonged to Anna and cut his carotid artery. When Walter Ross returned to the property, he found Walter Baldwin next to the dead body of his wife Anna, perhaps even hugging her, and this time Walter Baldwin was definitely dead.

Sheriff Wilson, together with Deputies Ted Crossley and Henry Nelson and coroner Dr. C.S. Dickson arrived at the scene in response to Walter Ross's phone call. The bodies of Anna and Walter Baldwin were taken to Flinn's Undertaking Parlor, where an inquest was held the next day, Saturday, the twentieth, at 10:00 a.m. The coroner's jury returned the expected verdict of murder-suicide. A service for Anna and Walter Baldwin was held in the chapel of Flinn's Undertaking Parlor at 10:00 a.m. on the following Monday with Reverend George Wixom of San Bernardino officiating. Anna and Walter were buried side by side at Evergreen Cemetery in Riverside. They rest together under one headstone. Anna's daughter Greta attended her mother and stepfather's funeral. She remembered seeing Walter Baldwin

Anna and Walter Baldwin were buried side by side in Evergreen Cemetery in Riverside. The birth year for Anna is incorrect. It should read "1883." *Courtesy Christine Brooks Ericson.*

in his casket with a bandage on his neck covering the injury he had supposedly inflicted on himself.

Certainly men have killed due to jealousy. It is undoubtedly believable that Walter Baldwin was driven to kill his wife in a jealous rage. That is the story that was passed down in Anna's family. One can only imagine how upset Walter was when he was told by the scheming Karl that Anna was having an affair with Mr. Slater. The local papers reported that Walter and Anna fought frequently. The only reason given was that her accent was hard for Walter to understand, and it made him angry. This seems improbable because Walter had known Anna for several months before their marriage and had to have known she had a heavy Swedish accent.

The part of this story that seems unbelievable is how Walter Baldwin died. Could a man really shoot himself three times and not kill himself? Then, could he get up, find a razor and kill himself by cutting his neck? Could he cut his neck and then walk over and lie down next to his dead wife? Or is it possible that brother-in-law Walter Ross, the only eyewitness to this unusual crime, had something to cover up by convincing the sheriff that Anna and Walter Baldwin's deaths were the result of a murder-suicide?

Any reports written about the deaths of the Baldwins by the officers at the scene have long since been relegated to the dustbin. We are just left with family stories and newspaper accounts. All of these stories are consistent with the account that Walter Baldwin shot his wife and then shot himself multiple times before he cut his own throat. It appears that Maude and Walter Ross had little to gain from the deaths of Anna and Walter Baldwin. The land the two couples were faming was leased, not owned. Anna and Walter Baldwin appeared to have few assets of any sort. The only thing Anna's daughter Greta received after her mother's death was Anna's clothing.

The Riverside County sheriff, two deputies and the county coroner all responded to the scene of the Baldwins' deaths. There was also an inquest held the next day where a coroner's jury could hear the evidence and see the victim's bodies. Presumably, most of the evidence both at the scene and as presented to the jury fit the story as reported by Walter and Maude Ross.

At the time of the Baldwins' deaths, Walter Ross was twenty-six years old, and Maude Ross was twenty-seven. Their five-year-old daughter Evelyn was presumably living with her parents. It is hard to imagine that they plotted to kill their relatives next door while their five-year-old daughter was about. We can't forget that Anna's family was also nearby, and it appears that Anna kept in regular contact with them. As a matter of fact, her sister Olga was the informant on Anna's death certificate.

As for the Rosses, the 1920 census indicated that two years after the Baldwins' deaths, the Rosses had moved to a nearby town, and Walter Ross was working as an auto mechanic. Ten years later, when the 1930 census was taken, they had moved to another nearby town, and Walter Ross was still working as an auto mechanic. Walter and Maude Ross seemed to be living an unremarkable life after the events of July 1918. It is difficult to tell from the census records, but they certainly did not seem to be wealthy. At best, they seemed to be middle class.

Almost one hundred years later, the facts and motives behind the deaths of Walter and Anna Baldwin still seem strange and even questionable. It seems unlikely that they were murdered by someone else, but we will probably never know exactly what caused the tragic deaths of Anna and Walter Baldwin on that hot July day in Glen Avon.

Chapter 11

The Curse of the Santa Ana River Bridge

It was a rough couple of years for trying to get across the Santa Ana River in 1916 and 1917. It seemed that everyone from Mother Nature to local pyromaniacs and perhaps even German saboteurs had it out for the bridge from West Riverside to Riverside.

The bridge across the Santa Ana River near Mount Rubidoux was an important crossing point. It was the main entrance into the city of Riverside from Los Angeles and all points west. Mission Boulevard took people to the West Riverside Bridge, and from there, they could travel into Riverside and to the east to Palm Springs and the Coachella Valley and to the south to San Diego. Having a safe and sturdy bridge at that point was a priority for both the city of Riverside and the county of Riverside. From a local standpoint, it was important because many people who lived in the Jurupa Valley area relied on that bridge to get to the neighboring city of Riverside to work, to attend church and to do shopping they couldn't do in Jurupa Valley.

The first bridge was constructed at that point on the river in the 1880s. It was nine hundred feet long with sixty-foot-wide spans. It was replaced in 1904–05 by a bridge made up of five iron spans of one hundred feet each. The water channel under that bridge was deepened, as it was thought that the deeper channel would allow better water flow during flood events. That was why the new bridge was four hundred feet shorter than the old bridge.

This 1911 photo shows the metal bridge built in 1904–05 across the main channel of the Santa Ana River. In the days before the river was controlled with levees, the river separated into two channels as it passed Mount Rubidoux. *Courtesy Riverside Metropolitan Museum.*

The problems with the bridge started with one of the epic floods the Santa Ana River is known for. An unprecedented amount of rain fell in January 1916. One hundred feet of road leading up to the bridge on the West Riverside side was washed away on January 16. The rain continued, and on January 18, at about 1:30 a.m., two spans of the bridge were washed out by the force of the water. Logs and railroad ties coming down the river likely contributed to the failure of the bridge.

A temporary footbridge was put in place by the Riverside Portland Cement Company. It allowed at least some travel between Riverside and West Riverside and also allowed the cement plant's employees in Riverside to be able to get to work. A temporary oiled-wood bridge was soon built in place of the portions of the bridge that had been washed out, at a cost of $5,900.

All was well again until April 1917. Contractor J.M. Hibbard of the Hibbard Bridge Company was at the site of the temporary bridge with a gang of men. They were there to remove a pile of unused lumber. As they worked to remove the lumber, they discovered a bulky package wrapped in a Los Angeles newspaper and tied with a tarred rope. Inside the package were seven sticks of dynamite and several blasting caps. The police were called, and their investigation determined that the dynamite

This photo shows the destructive force of the 1916 flood on the West Riverside Bridge that crossed the Santa Ana River between the Jurupa Valley area and the city of Riverside. *Courtesy Steve Lech.*

was to be used to blow up the bridge. The police notified federal authorities, and Secret Service agents came from Los Angeles to do their own investigation of the incident. Police and federal authorities in other cities were informed of the discovery of the explosives in case it was part of a larger plot by German saboteurs to blow up bridges in California.

On April 27, Harry H. Lange wrote a letter to the *Riverside Daily Press* proposing a theory concerning the dynamite that had nothing to do with alien enemies. Lange said he had been a member of the wrecking crew hired to dismantle the remaining two spans of the bridge after the flood in January 1916. After the bridge was dismantled, all but two of the crew moved to the Pedley Road crossing of the river to start erecting the remaining bridge spans to replace the Pedley bridge, which had also been washed away in the same flood. The remaining two men were tasked with blasting out the old concrete foundations of the West Riverside bridge. He suggested that instead of a Teutonic plot, the dynamite was just left over from that operation. The only problem with this theory is that there was no mention that the paper and rope used to package the dynamite and blasting caps looked like it had been in the weather for any length of time. The police also did not publicize the date on the *Los Angeles Times* used to wrap the dynamite. That piece of information could validate or refute Lange's theory.

Shortly thereafter, dynamite was discovered near two other bridges in Southern California. On June 17, dynamite was found under the Salt Lake Railway Bridge over the Los Angeles River. A night watchman saw a flickering light and, when he investigated, discovered a lit fuse with a stack of dynamite. On July 22, a box containing about seventy-five sticks of dynamite was found hidden in a bush near a railroad bridge in the Cajon Pass area of San Bernardino County. It is not known if any connection was ever made between the three incidents or if anyone was ever arrested for these crimes.

More than fifty incidences of sabotage occurred in the United States between 1914 and 1918. Targets were primarily sites that manufactured or stored military supplies, but railroad lines and bridges were also targets. The most infamous of these attacks was the destruction of the Black Tom Pier in New York Harbor, near Liberty Island. The pier area was home to many warehouses and ships that held explosives, munitions and fuel, which were being stored and readied for shipment to Europe. On July 30, 1916, several fires were set at the pier. This set off numerous explosions that continued through the night. The fire didn't stop raging until all of the explosives and fuel had been consumed. Shrapnel flew as far as a mile away, and thousands of windows in New York and New Jersey were broken by the explosions. Investigations done after the war laid the blame for this incident firmly with German saboteurs.

Two months after the dynamite was discovered, at 2:00 p.m. on June 17, 1917, a road worker discovered a small blaze on the West Riverside Bridge. He immediately extinguished the fire and stayed at the bridge for another twenty minutes to make sure the fire was out. No one thought anything of this event because the bridge was made of oil-soaked wood, and it was assumed that a spark from a passing car started the fire. A road foreman crossed the bridge at 3:00 p.m. and saw no sign of fire at that time.

However, less than an hour after the road foreman crossed the bridge, another fire was discovered at 3:50 p.m. This fire started in the middle of the bridge, and by the time it was discovered, it was significant enough to require an immediate call to the city fire department. The West Riverside

This early fire equipment was likely used to fight the fire that destroyed much of the West Riverside Bridge. *Courtesy Steve Lech.*

area on the west side of the bridge was unincorporated and did not have a fire department at that time. The city fire truck arrived promptly but found that it did not have enough hose on board to reach the bridge from the nearest fire hydrant at Sixth and Pepper Streets in Riverside. The truck sped back to the station and returned with more hose, but by that time, the bridge was fully engulfed in flame. After laying half a mile of hose, the firefighters put out the fire but were able to save only about fifty feet of the bridge, making it almost a total loss.

That evening, motorists who wished to get into Riverside or points east had to go back by way of Colton or drive through Pedley and take the Pedley Bridge into Arlington. The local newspapers reported that hundreds of motorists who had gone to Los Angeles and the beach that day were cut off from the west entrance into the city. Riverside County Supervisors approved plans for rebuilding on June 22, and another temporary bridge was opened on September 18. A permanent bridge was finally built in 1923. The West Riverside (now Rubidoux) Bridge has never suffered again another series of destructive or near destructive events like it did in 1916–17.

Chapter 12

Bad Blood Over Chickens May Have Led to Poisoning

Arthur J. Parks was the son of Arthur F. and Mary Ann Parks, one of the earliest pioneer families in the Jurupa Valley area. Arthur F. and Mary Ann were originally from England. Converted by Mormon missionaries, they immigrated to the United States, arriving in New Orleans in 1848. In 1851, they left in a wagon train from St. Louis to travel to Salt Lake City, Utah, and soon moved on to Cedar City, Utah. Their fourth child, Arthur, was born during the two years they resided there. The family moved to San Bernardino in 1855. Arthur F. Parks purchased fifty acres of land from Louis Robidoux on February 16, 1867, and purchased another sixty acres of land from Robidoux's son Pasqual on May 8 of the same year. In September 1867, just as Arthur J. was turning twelve years old, the Parks family moved on to their land in what is today the community of Rubidoux.

Arthur (from here on, "Arthur" refers to Arthur J. Parks) attended the Jurupa School, which was established in 1869. It was initially held in the Parks family home before a small adobe building was constructed for the school. Arthur's older brother Heber went to Los Angeles to attend business school, but it does not appear that Arthur had similar ambitions. It seems that when he became an adult he began farming. In 1891, a local newspaper mentioned that he had produced 3,600 trays of raisins on his ranch. He never married but was surrounded by the many family members who also lived in the Rubidoux area. Unlike his older brother

This photograph shows the Arthur Parks family, including Arthur (left center) and his wife, Mary Ann (right center). Their son Arthur J. Parks is in the bottom left-hand corner. *Courtesy Ida Parks Condit family.*

Heber, Arthur did not become involved in local politics and was never appointed to a county position nor ran for public office.

On the afternoon of Saturday December 29, 1900, Elmo Parks, the nineteen-year-old son of Heber Parks, said that he saw his Uncle Arthur go into the tent occupied by Byron Ferrell,* who worked as a hired hand on Arthur's place. A moment later Elmo heard his uncle drop something into a pail of water, followed by a sizzling noise. Elmo waited for his uncle to leave the tent and then immediately went inside and saw what looked like some sort of chemical in the bottom of the pail of water. This was the pail that Ferrell usually drank from. Later that evening, when Ferrell returned from his work, he was met near the tent by Elmo Parks, who told him what his Uncle Arthur had done.

* His first name was reported as both Byron and Hiram. His last name was spelled as Ferrell, Ferrall and Farrell in local papers.

After Elmo told him about Arthur putting something in his pail of water, Ferrell went into his tent to inspect the pail himself. He, too, saw some sort of substance in the bottom of the pail. Ferrell then came into Riverside to report the incident to the sheriff's department. One newspaper account said that Ferrell brought the pail with him to Riverside. Another said that Sheriff P.M. Coburn sent Deputy Sheriff Brown and Constable Scott the next day to investigate Ferrell's charges. They went to the tent, and in that report, the officers found both the pail and a container of poison and brought both back to Riverside.

However the pail got to Riverside, it and the container of poison were taken to Sebrall's drugstore. There, a clerk by the name of Jackson identified the substance as cyanide of potassium, a chemical commonly used in the fumigation of trees. One newspaper article said that there was enough poison in the water to kill a thousand men. The pail and the bottle of poison found next to it were given to the city marshal to hold on to, pending the outcome of the investigation.

On December 31, Ferrell came to town and swore the official complaint before Justice Mills, charging Arthur with putting poison in his water with the intent to poison him. A warrant was issued and given to Constable Scott to serve. Scott went to Arthur's place in West Riverside but discovered that he was in Riverside at William Preston's livery stable. Scott went to Preston's stable and there, sure enough, he found Arthur lying in a bed in the stables' office, very sick with the grippe. In the good old days, "grippe" was the name for influenza.

Arthur denied the whole affair and said Ferrell made it up out of spite. Friends of Arthur's said he wasn't near Ferrell's place on Saturday and so could not have put poison in the pail. The physicians attending Arthur forbade his being taken from bed. On January 2, the court officers went to the stables to arraign Arthur. He was placed under a $1,000 bond to guarantee his appearance in court in attempting to poison Ferrell. Arthur then hired attorney Lafayette Gill to defend him. The *Riverside Enterprise* said on January 3 that if "there is anyone who can clear him it will be Mr. Gill."

Two stories were floated as to why the poisoning may have occurred. One was that Ferrell and Mrs. Orlando Parks, wife of another of Arthur's brothers, had had a quarrel about some chickens, and Arthur took it upon himself to deal with the situation. The other story is that Arthur and Ferrell had some trouble brewing between then and had been on the outs for some time.

The case against Arthur Parks was called the afternoon of January 8 in Justice Mill's courtroom for the preliminary examination of Parks. District Attorney Evans asked for a continuance until the following day because two of the State's most important witnesses in this case, Elmo and Heber Parks, could not be found when the constable tried to subpoena them. The district attorney said that the case of the people could not be properly presented without them. The defendant's attorney, Mr. Gill, protested vigorously because all of the defendant's witnesses were present, but the judge did grant the postponement.

The next day, the preliminary examination before Judge Mills commenced. Four witnesses were sworn in. The first was the complainant, Ferrell. He told the story as had been reported previously in the local newspapers—about coming home and being told by Elmo Parks that there was poison in his pail of drinking water, put there by Arthur Parks. He admitted that he had no personal knowledge of who put the poison in his pail.

Heber Parks testified next. He said that his son Elmo told him that poison had been put in the pail of water and that he had come to town with his son, bringing the cyanide with them, which was then handed over to the sheriff. That was all he knew of the affair, he testified.

Sheriff Coburn testified that he had received the poison and that he had given it to Mr. Jackson, a clerk at Sebrall's drugstore. He personally did not know what the substance was but was told it was cyanide. The final witness was the drugstore clerk Mr. Jackson. He testified that he examined the substance brought in by Sheriff Coburn and that it was cyanide, a most deadly poison.

Elmo Parks had still not been found and subpoenaed to testify. Initially, District Attorney Evans asked for another continuance so that he could once again try to get Elmo, the most important witness in the case, to court to testify. But before the judge could rule on the request, Mr. Evans asked the court to dismiss the case and discharge the defendant because he did not believe it was possible to secure a conviction in this case. The court did as requested by Mr. Evans, and the case was discharged.

According to the *Riverside Enterprise* on January 10, 1901, "...and thus ended the seven days' wonder of West Riverside."

On January 10, the *Riverside Daily Press* reported, "It appears that Elmo Parks...is visiting a cousin at Avalon. It is thought he was not at all anxious to be present at the hearing, and found it convenient to be absent when he was most wanted." He was staying with his cousin Lance Bolton on Catalina.

After the alleged poisoning incident, Arthur Parks dropped out of the public eye, and his name rarely appeared in the local newspapers. The 1910 census indicated that he had moved to the Oak Glen area. He died December 23, 1916, at the age of sixty-three. He was buried in the Pioneer Cemetery in San Bernardino, the same cemetery where both of his parents were buried.

Elmo went on to marry Lulu May Sutter on June 21, 1905. They had three daughters. Their oldest, Dorothy, married John E. Cote, son of John and Grace Cote.

Chapter 13

Paydays Become Wild Times

It was a wild time in 1923 when the workers living in company housing at the Riverside Portland Cement Company got so rowdy on payday that the cement company finally had to call in the sheriff. The Cement Company employed about six hundred men at its plant on what is now Rubidoux Boulevard, just south of the county line. Hundreds of the employees were Mexican workers who lived in bunkhouses provided by the cement company. Gamblers, bootleggers and women of ill repute realized the bonanza awaiting them if they showed up to ply their trade and take advantage of the money that flowed on payday.

The Riverside Portland Cement Company began its Crestmore operation in 1906. The limestone deposits on the company's five-hundred-acre property provided the material to produce the cement needed to help build everything from houses to dams in booming Southern California and throughout the southwest. Hundreds of workers were needed by the company to fill jobs that included mining the limestone, hauling it to the rock crushers and then the kilns, mixing the cement and bagging it. In order to house the hundreds of mostly single men who worked at the plant, the company built bunkhouses adjacent to the cement works.

Irving Gill, considered to be one of California's most renowned and innovative architects, approached the owners of the Riverside Portland Cement Company in 1913 about designing barracks for its employees. Gill was as likely to use his skills as an architect designing a mansion

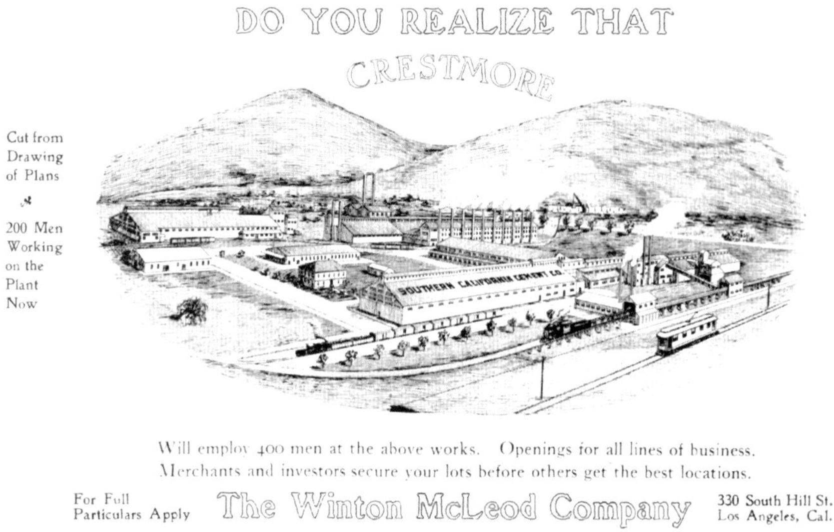

This advertisement for the Southern California Cement Company in Crestmore appeared in the May 24, 1907 issue of *As You Like It* magazine. In the middle left of the rendering appears to be the planned worker housing. *Courtesy Riverside Metropolitan Museum.*

for a wealthy client as housing for migrant workers. According to Bruce Kamerling in his book *Irving J. Gill, Architect* (1993), "As envisioned by Gill, the complex would have included two rectangular structures surrounded by trees with central courtyards...Gill intended to use the tilt-slab construction method, creating a continuous outside wall and a central garden. Apparently, Gill was unable to convince the company to go along with his full concept. The complex was finally constructed of wood but did have the amenities of a central garden with a covered pavilion."

In spite of Gill's efforts to provide pleasant housing for the cement plant's Mexican immigrant workers, the men, who spoke primarily Spanish, were left with little to do to fill their free time. At that time, the cement plant was fairly isolated from the surrounding cities of Riverside and San Bernardino. Besides, it is doubtful that the local cities would have welcomed hundreds of cement plant employees out to have a good time on payday. The men could have used the trolley that ran from the plant to Riverside to find recreation in that town, but Riverside's city fathers were a conservative group and would have frowned on an influx of Spanish-speaking workers. In stepped the gamblers, bootleggers and prostitutes.

After the request came from the cement company for help with the situation brewing in the workers' quarters, Sheriff Clem Sweeters planned the raid on the bunkhouses for the evening of September 6. Sweeters and Deputy Sheriffs George Swanson, Wesley Walrath, Paul Mapes and Sam Harbison conducted the raid. First, they quietly confronted Florena Reyes, a bootlegger who had set up shop on the hood of his Ford car. There he lined up dozens of pint bottles of illegal liquor (this was during Prohibition, don't forget) and sold them as fast as he was able to collect the three dollars per bottle that he charged his eager customers. The lawmen confiscated the unsold booze as well as Reyes's car and quietly ushered Reyes away to the county jail. The newspapers seem to have gotten Reyes's first name wrong. He was likely Florentino Reyes, a twenty-seven-year-old resident of San Bernardino.

Next, the sheriff and his men raided the poker game going on in one of the bunkhouses. The gamblers had spread a blanket out on the floor and were playing, many with piles of money in front of them. When the officers burst through the locked door, the men began grabbing for their money and cards. The deputies began grabbing for the money and cards, too. Deputy George Swanson was able to snatch a little over sixteen dollars, the most of any of the lawmen. Information was taken down on all twenty of the gamblers, but only three were transported to jail. The rest all had money on account with the cement company, so Sheriff Sweeters felt confident that the men would still be in the area when it came time to bring them to trial.

After the sheriff and his deputies were done with the gamblers, the officers then dealt with the women. Three women had been brought from Los Angeles to part the men from their money. Maria Hernandez, Nellie Gonzales and Fraise Narez were taken to jail by the officers.

The next day, Justice of the Peace H.C. Hibbard and his courtroom were engaged in dealing with the aftermath of the raid. First, Justice Hibbard dealt with the women, who turned out to be girls, really. The girls came to Crestmore from Los Angeles in a rented coupe, which could be gotten at that time for four dollars a day. All three said that they did not have any money, but the jail matron, Mrs. Swanson, found a string of gold pieces hanging around one girl's neck.

The girls pleaded guilty and asked to be sentenced at once. Justice Hibbard sentenced each to thirty days in jail but suspended their sentence on the condition that they leave Riverside within the hour and never return to Crestmore. If they were found at Crestmore again, Justice Hibbard said that they would receive six months in the county jail. The *Riverside Daily Press* said that a Mexican dandy was waiting to drive them back to Los Angeles. The youngest of the girls, who appeared to be about fifteen years old, said that the well-dressed man was her brother.

Reyes, the bootlegger, pled not guilty and was bound over to the higher court on a $1,000 bond. After thinking the issue over and, it was suspected, talking the situation over with higher-ups in his bootlegging organization, Reyes decided to plead guilty to the bootlegging charge. Justice Hibbard fined Reyes $500 and confiscated his car to be auctioned off at a sheriff's sale. Reyes didn't have the money to pay the fine but somehow put the word out about his predicament.

When the men at the Crestmore plant found out that their favorite bootlegger was stuck in jail because he couldn't pay his fine, a collection was started. It was assumed that the men wanted Reyes out of jail so he could once again ply his trade and supply them with illegal liquor. Before you know it, the full fine had been collected, with the understanding that the men's contributions would go toward their next purchase with Reyes.

A second bootlegger was also arrested in the raid, although the local newspapers didn't get wind of that until he appeared in court the next day. Camelio Rameriz had liquor in his possession and was selling it on the sly to the men at the Crestmore bunkhouses. Justice Hibbard also put him under a $500 bond and required Rameriz to answer for his crime in superior court. There was no report about a collection being taken up for Rameriz.

The three alleged gamblers who were among those caught enjoying the poker game during the raid were also required to put up a cash bond of fifty dollars each. Two of the men were Pedro Asores and Trino Rengil. The third man was not named in the newspaper.

After this raid, everyone involved felt sure that the payday orgies of wine, women and cards were over for the foreseeable future. Certainly, no more newspaper articles appeared later about similar raids.

Chapter 14

All-Housewife Jury Convicts Mistress of Manslaughter

The couple drove out from Los Angeles, leaving their swank apartment off Wilshire Boulevard, to spend the weekend at his 150-acre ranch with its spacious, showplace of a house. After they arrived, they settled into the lanai room to have a drink. The man had more than one and became intoxicated, as was later confirmed by the coroner. The woman, his companion and paramour of twelve years, had become weary of the problems they were having and, after trying for a while to appease him, finally gave into the fighting that seemed to happen so frequently. As he goaded her by showing her some glassware that was a gift from a Broadway actress, she told him to stop talking about it, while the housekeeper listened in on the fight from another room. At last, at about 6:00 p.m., she helped him downstairs to his bedroom suite. The arguing continued, and the gun on the nightstand was picked up. She said he threatened her with it, and as they struggled for the weapon, it went off. Her lover had nothing to say about the matter. He was dead.

According to the newspapers at the time, Agnes Garnier was an attractive brunette of fifty-three who managed the upscale DuBarry Apartment Hotel in Los Angeles. John E. Owen was a wealthy married attorney of sixty-eight who owned property in several states, was president of the National Apartments Owner's Association and was a past president of the Riverside Rotary Club. The connection between these two people began in 1937, when Owen hired Garnier to manage one of his Los Angeles apartment houses. The connection ended when Garnier shot Owen to death at his home on his Jurupa Hills Rancho in Glen Avon on April 22, 1949.

John Owen was a very wealthy man. He was an attorney in Detroit before he moved west in 1939. Owen even served a partial term in the Michigan Assembly in the 1920s. He invested in a number of apartment buildings in Los Angeles, including the upscale DuBarry Apartments. In addition to those buildings and the Glen Avon ranch, Owen owned the Rancho San Jacinto near Soboba Hot Springs, also in Southern California, and "vast ranch lands" in Arizona and Colorado. On his various ranches, he bred and raised Herford cattle and both thoroughbred and quarter horses. His wealth allowed him to travel among his various properties and to invest in his cattle and horse operations. In April 1945, he set a world record when he paid $30,000 for a Herford heifer. He regularly paid $20,000 or more for cattle to add to his breeding stock.

Owen married his wife, Florence, in 1929. He was forty-eight at the time, and she was thirty-five. They had one daughter, Doris Jane, who was born about 1931. The 1930 census said that it was the first marriage for both John and Florence. However, Owen had been married once before. He had an adult daughter, Madeline, from his first marriage. Madeline was married to Colonel Trippe, who was stationed at Camp Lee, Virginia, at the time of the incident. They had one daughter.

Agnes Garnier seemed to have a lot of men in her life that died young. The 1900 census shows three-year-old Agnes living with her mother and father, Mattie and A.W. Campbell, in Kansas City, Missouri. Sometime between 1900 and 1905, the Kansas State census shows that Mr. Campbell died and Agnes's mother was remarried to Robert Peterson. Later, the 1920 federal census lists Agnes, twenty-three, and already a widow, and her three-year-old son, Franklin Stephens, living with Agnes's mother and stepfather in Seattle, Washington. At this point, she was employed at a business college. By 1923, Agnes was remarried to James Garnier Sr. and gave birth that year to James A. Garnier Jr. She was again living in Missouri at that time.

In the 1930 census, Agnes was listed as manager of a good-sized hotel in Kansas City, Missouri. Both of her sons were living with her, and the census said she was married. However, her husband is not listed as living at the hotel with her and the children. No further information could be found for James Garnier Sr. According to the *Los Angeles Times*, she had been widowed for several years at the time of John Owen's death.

John Owen bought 150 acres in Glen Avon in the fall of 1944 and began immediately to put the property to use raising Herford cattle. An article in the April 17, 1945 edition of the *Los Angeles Times* discussed the expansion of John's herd of cattle at his Jurupa Hills Rancho. This expansion included the heifer for which he paid the world-record price. His ranch, located at the intersection of Mission Boulevard and Garnet Road (now Pedley Road), included the fields for the cattle, citrus groves and a house that was, by 1949 standards, quite the showplace.

The house was described in various articles in the *Los Angeles Times* and *Riverside Enterprise* as "palatial," a "mansion," "luxurious," "elaborately furnished," a "spacious, many roomed ranch" and it had "long been regarded as one of the show spots of Riverside County." It included a lanai room with a bar and a living room with a baby grand piano. A

John Owen's home is still located on the east side of Pedley Road, just south of the 60 freeway. *Courtesy author.*

study adjoined Owen's bedroom on the downstairs level. The walls of the study were lined with pictures of his prizewinning Herford cattle. The *Times* reported that Owen had paid over $500,000 for the place. The house still exists today, located on the side of a hill just south of the 60 freeway and just east of Pedley Road, looking down on the Bravo Mobile Home Park.

The paths of John E. Owen and Agnes Garnier crossed in 1937, when John hired Agnes to manage his Wilshire Towers apartments. On April 25, 1937, a classified ad for the Wilshire Towers Apartments ran in the *Times*. It said that the Wilshire Towers was "Beverly Hills newest, largest and most complete Apartment house." The building included an elevator, maid service and garages. The ad also called out Agnes Garnier

The Wilshire Towers in Beverly Hills was the first apartment house that Agnes Garnier managed for John Owen. *Courtesy author.*

Agnes Garnier managed the upscale DuBarry Apartments in the Wilshire area of Los Angeles for over ten years. *Courtesy author.*

as the manager of the building. Built in 1929, this apartment building is still located at 218 South Tower Drive.

Just a year later, Owen made Garnier manager of another of his properties, the DuBarry Apartments, located at 458 South Catalina Street in Los Angeles. This was a much larger and more upscale apartment building, located near the Wilshire financial area.

John left his wife and moved to the Wilshire Towers a few months after he hired Mrs. Garnier. After several months separation from his wife, he returned to the family home and lived there for the next seven years with his wife and young daughter. The couple separated again in 1944, but never divorced.

We don't know how John Owen and Agnes Garnier's day began on April 22. What we do know is that they left from Los Angeles about 3:00 p.m. to travel to the Jurupa Hills Rancho. Housekeeper Edna Austin had arrived at the house earlier in the day, at about 12:30 p.m., to prepare for their visit. When they arrived, Owen went down to his study for a

This photograph shows Highway 60 through Glen Avon, circa 1948. When John Owen and Agnes Garnier drove down this stretch of road, they knew they were almost to Owen's Jurupa Hills Rancho. *Courtesy Cates family.*

while, and Garnier went to the lanai room, where she read a newspaper. Owen came upstairs to the lanai room about 4:40 p.m. and began to pour himself a drink from a decanter of brandy Garnier had given him the previous Christmas. Garnier said something to him about the drink because it was before five and she wanted him to not drink so much. He poured himself a drink anyway and offered her one. She declined, but when he offered again a little later, she accepted.

They went into the dining room about 5:30 p.m. for dinner, and as Austin was serving it to the pair, they were involved in a heated discussion in which "glasses" were mentioned a number of times. After dinner, the couple went downstairs to the study where, Austin believed, the conversation about the glasses continued. Garnier mentioned to the sheriff's deputies that Owen had returned recently from New York, where actress Irene Rich had given him a set of large heavy glasses decorated with Cossack figures for his birthday. A little before 6:00 p.m., Garnier and Owen came into the kitchen, and Owen told Austin to call ranch manager Pete Corrales because Garnier wanted to go home. Garnier protested that Owen was actually sending her away, and Owen repeated that it was actually Garnier that wished to leave. The couple returned downstairs to Owen's bedroom and study area, and while Austin was clearing the dining room table, she could hear more loud conversation coming from the couple. Austin heard the word "gun" once or twice. Austin agreed that Owen had been drinking that night and was "a little under the influence."

At first, when Austin heard the single shot, she thought it was a sound coming from the radio. Then moments after the shot sounded, shortly after 6:00 p.m., Garnier appeared at the top of the stairs and said, "I shot Mr. Owen." Austin raced downstairs and knelt by Owen. She told Garnier to call Pete Corales and to call a doctor and an ambulance, which Garnier did. Meanwhile, Austin tried to staunch the bleeding from the wound on Owen's torso under his left arm. Corales arrived very soon and also began trying to stop Owen's bleeding.

When the ambulance arrived, Owen was found still alive in a pool of blood on the floor of his bedroom. He was loaded into the ambulance but died en route to Riverside Community Hospital. Sheriff's Inspector Mel Vivion and Deputy Sheriff Gene Crumley reached the scene and found Garnier sitting in a chair. She refused to answer the officer's questions and just kept repeating that the shooting was an accident. A .32 revolver was at the scene, the same gun that ranch manager Corales later testified that he had given Owen and that Owen kept on his nightstand, next to his bed. News of the murder caused a large crowd of curiosity-seekers to gather at the ranch, and Sheriff Carl Rayburn ordered a guard stationed to keep people away.

By the day after the death of Owen, Garnier had retained the services of Hollywood attorney Sam Houston Allen, a descendant of the Sam Houston who figured so prominently in the history of Texas. Allen released a statement from Garnier that related her account of the shooting on April 22. She said that Owen had told the servants that Garnier was going to go back to Los Angeles but then told Garnier that if she left, he would shoot her. He suddenly grabbed the gun that was on his nightstand and lunged toward Garnier. After that, Garnier said she was not sure what happened. The next moment that she was clear about in her own mind was the moment when Owen fell to the ground.

An inquest was held Monday, April 25, and after less than forty-five minutes of testimony, the coroner's jury, consisting of nine men, returned with the verdict that Owen died as a result of a gunshot fired by Garnier. It was not up to the coroner's jury to determine guilt, just how the victim died.

John E. Owen was buried in Riverside's Olivewood Cemetery. *Courtesy Christine Brooks Ericson.*

The next day, Garnier was arraigned. Ironically, the arraignment occurred at almost the same time as Owen's funeral. The funeral was held at Simon's Mortuary, which was just across Eleventh Street from the courthouse. The pallbearers were members of the Riverside Rotary Club. Approximately one hundred people attended Owen's funeral. There were dozens of floral pieces, including one that was fashioned as a Rotary Club wheel. After the service, Owen was buried in Riverside's Olivewood Cemetery.

Law enforcement officials decided to take the step of convening a grand jury in the case. The grand jury heard witnesses and testimony from officers and the coroner. On April 30, the grand jury indicted Garnier, which sent her case straight to superior court for an arraignment. By this point, her two sons had arrived to offer their support. Her oldest son, Franklin Stephens, came from Lincoln, Nebraska, and younger son, James Garnier Jr., came from Kansas City, Missouri.

At her May 9 arraignment in superior court, Garnier entered a plea of not guilty. As she was entering her pleas, the transcript from the grand jury hearing was filed with the county clerk. That was the first chance the public and newspapers had to read about the testimony that had been given before the grand jury and would likely again be given in Garnier's trial. At the grand jury hearing, ranch foreman Pete Corales testified that Garnier had threatened Owen's life two weeks before his death, saying, "If I can't have him, no one else would." At that same time, when Garnier had stopped by the ranch on the way from Palm Springs to Los Angeles, she told Pete that she had traced calls Owen had made and they were going to the Waldorf Astoria Hotel in New York, where she knew Irene Rich was staying.

Newspapers across the country speculated that actress Irene Rich would figure prominently in the trial of Garnier, and they thought Rich might even be subpoenaed to testify. Rich, who was fifty-eight at the time of the shooting, had had some success in silent films but, in spite of having a good voice, only had small roles in talkies. She found success on the radio, where she had her own show for over ten years. She also did some stage work and was appearing in a play on Broadway when the shooting occurred.

Rich owned a ranch in the nearby Southern California town of Etiwanda and knew Owen due to their mutual interest in the ranching business. She often saw him when he came to the east coast on business as president of the National Apartment Owner's Association. However, Rich knew Owen was married and insisted that, after three failed marriages of her own, she was not interested in marrying again. However, just a year later, in 1950, Rich married her fourth husband and retired from acting. Rich did not end up having a prominent role in the trial of Garnier and was never subpoenaed to testify.

The jury selection process began on June 2. The defense and prosecution examined thirty-two possible jurors and used a total of seventeen peremptory challenges before settling on twelve women for the jury. Reporters called it the "all-housewife jury."

The *Los Angeles Times* described the attorneys and the judge in this trial. The head attorney for the prosecution was District Attorney William O. Mackey, who the *Times* described as a short, stocky man with a mane of white hair, who moved and talked with deliberate quiet. Assistant District Attorney Ray Sullivan was also part of the prosecution team. The *Times* said he was Mackey's opposite—tall, thin and bespectacled, with a drawly way of talking and a less reserved personality.

Sam Houston Allen, chief counsel for the defense, was, according to the *Times*, a Hollywood attorney who was a veteran of criminal trials and a man who used his impressive oratory in court. His associate was William Shaw, a young Riverside attorney. Shaw also had a resonant voice, and he moved with quick confidence.

The judge for the case, Russell Waite, was described in the *Times* as a tall, poised man of forty-four who had graying hair but looked younger than he was. He took office in January 1947 and was, at that time, the youngest superior court judge in California. Judge Waite's courtroom was one of the largest in the state, with a seating capacity of 143. All of those seats were filled every day of the trial.

The trial began on June 7. Minutes before Garnier entered the courtroom, she was served with legal papers from attorneys for Florence Owen, John Owen's widow. Mrs. Owen was demanding Garnier return a diamond ring Owen had given her that was supposedly worth $10,000. Garnier said he had given her the ring as a gift on her fiftieth birthday. She was wearing the ring the night that Owen was shot, and it was in the possession of the sheriff's department.

The prosecution elicited testimony from acquaintances of Garnier that she had mentioned that Owen was getting old and crabby. She told friends that she was thinking of getting her real estate broker's license and leaving him. Their intimate relationship had ended about three years before, due to the aging Owen's physical condition. It was suggested by her attorneys that this was what was making Owen difficult to get along with.

The prosecution tried to show that Owen was about to fire Garnier from her position as both his girlfriend and as his manager of the DuBarry Apartments. This possibility of losing her job and her jealousy of Owen's relationship with actress Irene Rich is what led to Owen's death, the prosecution claimed. Pete Corales, the ranch manager, testified that in early April, he and Garnier had a conversation in which she told Corales in a bitter tone, "if I can't have him, no one else will." Others testified about the fights Owen and Garnier had and the many times he threatened to fire her.

The defense chose to counteract the prosecution's witnesses through the reading of love letters Owen had sent Garnier through the years, to prove his love and devotion to her. Her attorneys put Garnier on the stand and then read more than twenty love letters, most of which were written from Owen to Garnier when she was on a trip to Honolulu in 1947. She wept quietly as the notes were read. The *Los Angeles Times* reported various quotes from the letters: "I have counted the hours and days since you left." "There has been no blonde." "If I were at all interested in blonds I wouldn't be so damn anxious to see you." "Did you get rid of your cold? I was more worried than you know about it." "I think you are a wonderful manager…I trust you fully in every way…I think you're a peach…I'm damned lonesome—FOR YOU…I've told you that before—remember????"

One letter that was read was written by Owen to Garnier only three days before his death.

> *My dear, never in my whole life has anyone meant what you have to me. That feeling can never change. I realize I am a different man. Something is wrong with me and I know it only too well. Personally I feel I shall gradually grow worse until I am a complete wreck. No longer do I have control over myself. At times I feel I will go wild. Maybe it would be better for all if I did. Anyway, no matter what may happen I shall always love you with all my heart and soul. Please always remember—this is and always will be my feeling for you.*

After closing arguments in which the defense referred to Garnier as Owen's "unwed wife" and the prosecution pushed for second-degree murder, the twelve women jurors began deliberations. The jury deliberated for just seven hours and thirty-four minutes. The verdict was read at 10:25 p.m. on June 17. The all-women jury decided that Agnes Garnier had committed manslaughter when she shot John Owen. One juror was seen weeping in the corridor outside the courtroom after the verdict. A week and a half later, Judge Waite sentenced Garnier to the sentence prescribed by law—one to ten years—and ordered her to the women's state prison in Tehachapi.

Prior to being sent to prison to begin her sentence, Garnier was allowed to go to Los Angeles to deal with some personal business. Accompanying her was her attorney Sam Houston Allen as well as Deputy Sheriffs Alice Shetlin and Mel Vivion. She was also accompanied by a reporter for the *Los Angeles Times*. Garnier went through her personal belongings looking for the holographic will that she insisted Owen had read to her two days before he was killed. She looked though crates of business and personal paperwork that was boxed up and in a storage facility but was not successful in locating it. She told the reporter that her conscience did not bother her.

Her attorney filed numerous appeals on her behalf, but none overturned her sentence. She began serving her sentence less than two weeks after her original conviction. While she was sentenced to a one to ten year term, at that time it was the California Adult Authority that set the length of term after the person began serving their sentence. Garnier was released from prison on May 8, 1951 after serving less than twenty-three months.

What ever happened to Agnes Garnier? At the time she was released from prison, it appears that her younger son James was living in San Diego, California. It seems that Garnier moved to that city as well. Social Security death records indicate that she died in January 1990 at the age of ninety-two in San Diego. Various public records indicate that her son James was still living in San Diego at the time as well.

Selected Bibliography

Brown, John, Jr., and James Boyd. *History of San Bernardino and Riverside Counties*. Chicago: Lewis Publishing Company, 1912.

Condit, Ida Parks. *Jurupa Peace and Friendship*. Riverside, CA: self-published, 1984.

Fitch, Robert J. *Profile of a Century—Riverside County, California, 1893–1993*. Riverside, CA: Riverside County Historical Commission Press, 1993.

Flacco, Anthony. *The Road Out of Hell: Sanford Clark and the True Story of the Wineville Murders*. New York, NY: Sterling Publishing Co., 2009.

Gunther, Jane Davies. *Riverside County, California Place Names*. Riverside, CA: Rubidoux Printing Company, 1984.

Johnson, Kim Jarrell. *Jurupa*. Charleston, SC: Arcadia Publishing, 2005.

———. *Rubidoux*. Charleston, SC: Arcadia Publishing, 2007.

Kamerling, Bruce. *Irving J. Gill, Architect*. San Diego, CA: San Diego Historical Society, 1993.

Kirby, Ruth A. *Ghost Towns of the Jurupa Mountains*. Riverside, CA: Jurupa Mountains Cultural Center, 1969.

Kurz, Don. *Rubidoux Rancho on the Jurupa*. Riverside, CA: self-published, 1972.

Lech, Steve. *Along the Old Roads*. Riverside, CA: self-published, 2004.

Patterson, Tom. *A Colony for California*. Riverside, CA: Press-Enterprise Company, 1972.

Paul, James Jeffery. *Nothing is Strange with You*. N.p.: Xlibris, 2008.

About the Author

Kim Jarrell Johnson is a lifelong resident of Jurupa Valley. She has written two books on the history of the Jurupa area: *Jurupa* and *Rubidoux*, and she coauthored *Riverside's Mission Inn* with Steve Lech. She writes a regular weekly history column for the *Riverside County Record* newspaper. A graduate of the University of California, Riverside, she went on to receive a master's degree in public administration at California State University, Fullerton. Kim lives in the Indian Hills area of Jurupa Valley with her husband of over twenty-five years, whom she first met in chemistry class at Rubidoux High School, and their two daughters.